# Who Was Karl Marx?

Joaquin:                                    11/19/21

Hope you find this short read
of interest.

Best!

*[signature]*

# Who Was Karl Marx?

The Men, the Motives and the Menace Behind Today's Rampaging American Left

By James Simpson

ISBN 9798513003151


Simpson Publishing

Baltimore, MD

To My Children

# Table of Contents

# Introduction

The Left is rampaging across our nation. Portland, Oregon is burning and many other cities face continuous looting, rioting and destruction. Literal miles of Minneapolis, Minnesota have been destroyed. Democrat-run cities are hemorrhaging people—fleeing for the relative sanity of red states. And while the Antifa/Black Lives Matter mob is wreaking havoc, destroying businesses and neighborhoods, leaders in those communities have taken an inexplicable hands-off attitude, even to the point of restraining a police response. Following the accidental police shooting of Daunte White in a Minneapolis, Minnesota neighborhood and generalized unrest over the Derek Chauvin trial, Minneapolis police and National Guard troops were targeted in a drive-by shooting. [1]

Today, George Floyd has assumed hero status, with huge murals erected in cities throughout the country. Is he worthy of it? Floyd did have an unfortunate life. A gifted athlete in his youth, Floyd squandered that opportunity through drug abuse. He was arrested and incarcerated multiple times, including a five-year sentence for robbery in which he pressed a gun to the female robbery victim's abdomen. He tried to turn his life around but never was able to quit the drugs. [2] During the arrest leading to his death he was high on multiple drugs, including a mega dose of deadly Fentanyl. This, plus his underlying health condition were major contributing factors, if not the reason he died.

George Floyd's death turbocharged a movement already very active during President Trump's entire tenure. Their reaction was not a surprise to analysts familiar with the radical Left's modus operandi. They were just waiting for such an opportunity. Floyd's death, while tragic, was nothing more than a pretext for unrestrained violence.

As a result, America today is virtually unrecognizable from a year ago. Democrat leaders have stood idly by or actually contributed to the atmosphere of hatred and chaos, both in their rhetoric and policy proposals. Misinformation from the press, politicians and even health officials has contributed to the deaths of over 600,000 Americans from COVID-19, despite former President Trump's relentless efforts to provide needed supplies and hospital beds, and unprecedented success in bringing antidotes to the market in record time. The new administration of Joe Biden has reversed every single successful policy of the Trump administration that brought unprecedented economic revitalization across America and stemmed the flow of illegal immigration.

Today there is an unprecedented illegal immigration crisis at our southern border, deliberately instigated by Biden and the Democrats. Prices are rising and Biden administration economic policies threaten to kill millions of jobs. Meanwhile, poisonous Critical Race Theory and Black Lives Matter rhetoric is being mainstreamed into public school curriculums, teaching children to hate America. At the same time, those same children are being indoctrinated to believe they can change sexual identity at will, in some cases without parental permission. The entire world seems to be going insane. And if this trend is not reversed, our nation and the world will face a cataclysm of biblical proportions.

Before we start, there are four fundamental concepts you need to understand:

1. "<u>The issue is never the issue. The issue is always the Revolution</u>." Former radical David Horowitz quoted another 60s radical here. What he meant was that no matter what the issue, be it gay and "transgender" rights, civil rights, immigrant rights, welfare rights, "social justice," "equity" or whatever buzzwords they use, the issue is only relevant insofar

as it can advance the "Revolution." And what is the Revolution? It is the Left's relentless goal to overthrow the existing order to achieve absolute power and the wealth that comes with it, *nothing else*.

2. <u>This is an asymmetric strategy of military conquest</u>. Stop thinking of our political controversies as simply differences of opinion between right and left. We are actually witnessing a Communist overthrow of the United States in real time. This sounds like a conspiracy theory, but it is not. Communists base their strategies on Sun Tzu's *Art of War*. Sun Tzu says "all war is deception," and the ultimate victory is to win without firing a shot. Instead of attacking the U.S. at its strength, i.e., with conventional arms, they attack us through our vulnerabilities: our freedom, our open society, our generous natures and willingness to "play fair." Ironically, those same concepts that gave us the freest, most generous, wealthiest nation in history, have left us vulnerable to attack by unscrupulous people willing to exploit them for their evil purposes.

3. <u>There is a method to the madness</u>. Every day we are subjected to mind-numbing lies and demonstrations of hypocritical double-standards by media, Hollywood, Big Tech, the political Left and certain circles in law enforcement. Down is up, right is wrong, truth is a lie, black is white. We often hear quotes from Orwell's *1984* and *Animal Farm* to describe what is happening. Normal people are baffled by its seeming illogic. But it has a deadly logic: to unhinge our society from any and all anchors to reality, stability and security, to strike fear into our hearts, and to make us desperate for it to stop. I call it *psychological terrorism*.[3] It is one of the most important unacknowledged reasons why Joe

Biden is President. The Left created absolute chaos for the Trump administration's four years. Despite Trump's delivering on unprecedented promises, many voted for Biden simply because they believed that by acquiescing to the Left and electing Biden it would end. Instead, he has ramped up the madness.

4. <u>At its heart, this evil agenda is Satanic</u>. Leftists run the gamut from well-meaning liberals thinking the Democrat Party is "compassionate," to hardcore Stalinists using every malicious tactic they can dream up to seize power. The core of the agenda, however, can only be described as Satanic, and a case can be made that many communists are not even atheists, but actually Satanists.

So where did this all come from? How did we get to this point? This short book will explain it all, and provide you with the weapons you need to confront it. It is actually nothing new. Every single radical agenda at work in the world today comes directly from the mind and work of Karl Marx. It is important, therefore, to ask the question: who was Karl Marx, who were the men that advanced his plan, and what have they done to achieve it?

# Who Was Karl Marx?

*"With disdain I will throw my gauntlet*
*full in the face of the world,*
*And see the collapse of this pygmy giant*
*Whose fall will not stifle my ardour.*
*Then I will wander godlike and victorious*
*Through the ruins of the world*
*And, giving my words an active force,*
*I will feel equal to the Creator."*
– Karl Marx.

We are all driven by fantasies. We fantasize wealth, happy and prosperous families, successful careers, love, friendship, popularity, completing our "bucket list"— any number of things. Some fantasies are temporal; some spiritual. Some are realistic; some not so much. Fantasies are so appealing because one can completely ignore those pesky complications that living in the real-world present. Hard experience and maturity force us to adjust, recognizing there are always tradeoffs. We modify our plans, forestalling some, abandoning others, and redouble our efforts when the goal appears possible.

Not so the Left. Their profound arrogance allows them to fantasize a future world unlike any other, one that requires the entire world's participation, willing or otherwise. It is a fantasy world where everyone shares the wealth equally; a world where unselfishness, peace and harmony reign. It is a world inspired by the noble-sounding cause of "social justice."

Yet it is a vision crammed with irony. Leftists lure prospective followers by appealing to their basest instincts of greed and envy, promising unearned material benefits confiscated from the "greedy rich." They aim to achieve their egalitarian utopia[4] by using the power of government to take property from those who earned it, giving it to those who didn't, and criticizing as "selfish" anyone who objects. Those purveyors of "injustice"—landlords, Wall Street, Big Oil, the NRA, tea partyers and other suspects—all the symbols of "capitalist oppression" finally get their comeuppance. Meanwhile, much of the stolen property winds up in the hands of the leftists themselves. They carve out exclusive, elite lifestyles with the spoils, but bristle at the suggestion that they are hypocritical.

No real effort is required to adopt this ideology, no rigorous education, no careful evaluation of facts. Just make bold, radical, self-righteous pronouncements and the Left establishment will welcome you with open arms and perhaps a job to boot. Leftists elevate themselves above the rest of humanity simply by donning the "progressive" mantle. It is why groups like Antifa and Black Lives Matter thrive today. They consider themselves frontline warriors in a battle for "fairness" and "social justice," without for a second considering what those words really mean. And the reality is stunning. More helpless, unarmed blacks have been murdered as the result of Antifa/BLM riots in 2020, than those killed by police that the rioters are supposedly protesting. But no matter, facts are no impediment to the noble mission.

These champions of equality fawn over their secular leaders—turning them into icons, complete with posters, symbols and slogans. The endpoint is a cult of personality as existed in Germany's Nazi regime under Adolf Hitler, Stalin's Soviet Union, Mao's China, Ho Chi Minh's North Vietnam, Saddam Hussein's Iraq, et cetera, and still exists in places like Communist Cuba and North Korea. So much for equality. And it is nothing new. It is ego-driven, arrogant immaturity, evident in youth of all generations, but persisting only in those adults who refuse to grow up.

Former President Obama personifies the modern progressive. Recall this quote from his 2008 ~~election~~ victory speech, "[G]enerations from now, we will be able to look back and tell our children that... This was the moment when the rise of the ocean began to slow, and our planet began to heal."[5] That has to be one of the most megalomaniacal statements any U.S. politician—drunk or sober—has ever made. It drips with self-aggrandizing conceit. It is difficult to believe he actually said it, and one is only convinced by watching the speech over and over again on YouTube. The only thing more frightening than this infantile display of arrogance is the fact that he was elected at all. And when he spoke this line, the wild audience response was reminiscent of a Hitler rally in old Nazi propaganda newsreels.

P.J. O'Rourke says: "At the core of liberalism is the spoiled child—miserable, as all spoiled children are, unsatisfied, demanding, ill-disciplined, despotic and useless. Liberalism is a philosophy of sniveling brats."[6]

That about sums it up. But perhaps we shouldn't besmirch the ideology simply because so many of its adherents are so personally repulsive. Let's look instead at the man who created it. Call it "Marxism," "communism," "socialism," "progressivism," or any of several other euphemisms, it reflects the beliefs, thought processes and personality of the man who popularized communism, Karl Marx.

It turns out that progressivism's end product is merely the reflection of Marx's personality, played out to devastating effect on the world stage. And we are seeing its reality every day now.

Like most leftist myths—manmade global warming, American "imperialism," capitalist "oppression," systemic racism, and all the evils attributed to America—Marx himself was the biggest

3

fraud of all. He has been built up by a century of propaganda into a kind of omniscient, benevolent god, but the man himself was hypocritically greedy, petty, arrogant, lazy, selfish, dishonest, two-faced, lecherous, bigoted and brimming with hatred—all the ugly characteristics he attributed to others to excuse the destruction he intended to inflict on the world.

Marx called blacks, "idiots" and "n*ggers;" Slavs were "ethnic trash" who only had "the immediate task of perishing in the revolutionary world storm;" Germans were "stupid people" who could only be redeemed by beating.[7] He called the proletariat he supposedly championed, "stupid boys, rogues, asses." Marx reviled Jews, even though he was ethnically Jewish himself. Marx supported slavery in America. He may have developed his resentment against capitalism as the result of his inveterate gambling in the stock market, where he frequently lost.[8] He had even been a paid informant for the German government, spying on his revolutionary friends.[9]

Marx wasn't even a Communist at first. "Commune-ism" was originally used to describe the ideology that inspired early communes in France. The term had been in circulation for at least a decade before Marx converted.[10] And though he would later claim that he was the only authentic Communist, in his early writings he rejected it entirely, adding, "Attempts by masses to carry out Communist ideas can be answered by a cannon as soon as they become dangerous..."[11] He should know. Despite all this, Marx became communism's most successful salesman.

Though born of Jewish parents, early in his life Marx was, ironically, raised as a Christian. His father had converted to Christianity shortly before Marx's birth in 1818 as a practical move to practice law in Lutheran-dominated Germany, where Jews were legally prohibited from practicing their professions.[12] Marx's high school writings suggest a strong Christian influence. His graduation essay was titled "On the Union of the Faithful with Christ." Here is a quote:

> *Thus, union with Christ consists in the most intimate, most vital communion with Him, in having Him before our eyes and in our hearts, and being so imbued with the highest love for Him, at the same time we turn our hearts to our brothers whom He has closely bound to us, and for whom also He sacrificed Himself.*
>
> *But this love for Christ is not barren, it not only fills us with the purest reverence and respect for Him, it also causes us to keep His commandments by sacrificing ourselves for one another, by being virtuous, but virtuous solely out of love for Him. (John 15: 9, 10, 12, 13, 14.)*[13]

But soon after high school, Marx turned away from Christianity and his writings became conspicuously anti-God—some have even suggested Satanist—and violent. Note the poem quoted at the beginning of this chapter. Marx reveals to the world that *he was not an atheist. He actually believed in God*, but rather than dismiss God as a myth, Marx sought to replace him. Note how closely his poem challenging God tracks with how God described Satan in Isaiah 14:

> *For you have said in your heart,*
> *I will ascend into heaven,*
> *I will exalt my throne above the stars of God;*
> *I will also sit on the mount of the congregation*
> *On the farthest sides of the north;*
> *I will ascend above the heights of the clouds,*
> *I will be like the Most High;* (Isaiah 14:13-14, NKJV).

As Communist-turned-whistleblower, Whittaker Chambers explained in his famous book, *Witness*:

*It is the great alternative faith of mankind. Like all great faiths, its force derives from a simple vision. Other ages have had great visions. They have always been different versions of the same vision: the vision of God and man's relationship to God. The Communist vision is the vision of Man without God. It is the vision of man's mind displacing God as the creative intelligence of the world.* [14]

Whether Marx knew it or not, he was preaching Satanism.

## A Penchant for Destruction

Marx and his comrades were not so much interested in building as they were in destroying. Marx adored the Mephistopheles quotation from Faust, "Everything in existence is worth being destroyed." [15] One of his early co-conspirators, the anarchist Mikhail Bakunin, proclaimed: "In this revolution we will have to awaken the Devil in the people, to stir up the basest passions. Our mission is to destroy, not to edify. The passion of destruction is a creative passion." [16]

Marx predicted worldwide calamity from the revolution he hoped to foment:

*A silent, unavoidable revolution is taking place in society, a revolution that cares as little about the human lives it destroys as an earthquake cares about the houses it ravages. Classes and races that are too weak to dominate the new conditions of existence will be defeated.* [17]

The *Communist Manifesto* he co-authored with Friedrich Engels in 1848 makes it explicit:

*The Communists disdain to conceal their views and aims. They openly declare that their ends can be attained only by the forcible overthrow of all existing social conditions.*[18]

In 1848 the Austrian Empire put down a series of revolutionary movements. Reacting to this in an essay titled "The Victory of the Counter-Revolution in Vienna," Marx concluded: "... there is only one way in which the murderous death agonies of the old society and the bloody birth throes of the new society can be shortened, simplified and concentrated, and that way is revolutionary terror."[19]

Marx was not interested in the "oppressed of the earth." He was neither compassionate nor egalitarian. One of his contemporaries, Giuseppe Mazzini, said that he was:

> *[A] destructive spirit whose heart was filled with hatred rather than love of mankind... Despite the communist egalitarianism which [Marx] preaches he is the absolute ruler of his party... and he tolerates no opposition.*[20]

Engels recorded his first impressions of Marx:

> *He does not walk or run, he jumps on his heels and rages full of anger as if he would like to catch the wide tent of the sky and throw it to the earth. He stretches his arms far away in the air; the wicked fist is clenched, he rages without ceasing, as if ten thousand devils had caught him by the hair.*[21]

Bakunin said of Marx, "One has to worship Marx in order to be loved by him. One has at least to fear him in order to be tolerated by him. Marx is extremely proud, up to dirt and madness.[22]

# A Greedy, Parasitic Slob

The picture that emerges is one of a greedy, selfish, whining, megalomaniacal egotist, the grown-up version of a severely spoiled brat. In youth he was well cared for by his wealthy father. While at school he received an allowance exceeding the average income of 95 percent of Germany's population at the time.[23] Later in life he hovered over ailing relatives like a vulture, impatiently waiting for them to die to learn what, if anything, he would inherit. Upon the death of his wife's uncle, he wrote to Engels:

> *Yesterday we were informed of a very happy event, the death of my wife's uncle, aged 90. As a result, my mother-in-law will save an annual impost of 200 talers and my wife will get almost £100; more if the old dog hasn't made over to his housekeeper such of his money as is not entailed...*[24]

Francis Wheen's biography of Marx states that, "Relations with his mother were icy and distant, not least because she had been inconsiderate enough to stay alive and thus keep the rebellious heir from his inheritance."[25] Following her death on November 30, 1863, Marx hurried off to see about it. He wrote to his wife on December 15th:

> *What she gave Conradi [their attorney] was a notarial copy of a sort of will, which contained nothing but the following terms: 1. She left all the furniture and linen to Emilie with the exception of the gold - and silverware; 2. To her son Carl [sic] she leaves the 1,100 talers, etc.; 3. To Sophie, father's portrait. That's all there is to the will...*

He complained that:

> *As yet, I know nothing about the actual value of the estate, because all the papers are in the sealed cupboard. The seals have not yet been removed because of the time-consuming formalities... Besides, there's nothing left here in Trier (Grünberg was sold long ago) except 5 casks of 1858 wine, which my mother refused to sell at the right moment, and some gold and silverware. This will be shared*

*out equally among the heirs. The real assets, however, are all in Uncle's hands.*[26]

He added that he would next be visiting his Aunt Esther in Frankfurt, and made a point of mentioning that another aunt living with her was rich.[27]

More than one biographer has noted Marx's poor hygiene and slovenly habits. As described in a New York Times book review:

*Here is a man never more passionate than when attacking his own side, saddled with perennial money problems and still reliant on his parents for cash, constantly plotting new, world changing ventures yet having trouble with both deadlines and personal hygiene, living in rooms that some might call bohemian, others plain "slummy," and who can be maddeningly inconsistent when not lapsing into elaborate flights of theory and unintelligible abstraction.*[28]

Marx's father was generous with him to a fault and treated him as an equal, but apparently Marx was unimpressed:

*While his mother nagged him (to no avail) to change his underwear at least once a week, his father treated his brilliant, self-confident son as an intellectual equal. By the time Marx was a 19-year-old, beer-swilling, dueling university student and spendthrift, his father, then dying of tuberculosis, admitted: "I can only propose, advise. You have outgrown me." Marx returned the compliment by skipping his father's funeral a year later.*[29]

Marx's economic theories had no grounding in reality. He had no experience actually working in the real world and lacked understanding of basic economic principles. In a way, that was an advantage, because he was then free to dream up absurd economic theories that, he promised, would usher in an earthly paradise. "Workers of the world unite," Marx proclaimed, "You have nothing to lose but your chains."

Instead, Marxism has enslaved almost half of the world—those who survived, that is. Soberly analyzed, his agenda could have only one predictable result: centralization of power and wealth in the hands of the top leaders of the state. And when entire societies are denied property, income and the means for productive enterprise, even survival, they tend to revolt. So totalitarian, repressive government is a predictable outcome. Indeed, it is essential to protect those at the top. The *Communist Manifesto* is more a reflection of Marx the man, his towering pride, his greedy ambition, and his contempt for the world, than a pamphlet offering any solutions to mankind.

In his book *Intellectual Morons*, Daniel Flynn quotes British writer Paul Johnson who observed, "Marx never set foot in a mill, factory, mine, or other industrial workplace in the whole of his life." Flynn observes "His war against free enterprise stemmed not from solidarity with the workers but from his constant debts, unemployment, and inability to support his family. His mother complained, 'Karl should accumulate capital instead of just writing about it.'"[30]

Marx's personal life may jam open a window into his tormented soul. Two of his daughters and a son-in-law committed suicide. Three children died of malnutrition. He had an illegitimate child by his maid, but said that Engels, a bachelor, was the father. Engels agreed to raise the child as his own and kept the truth a secret until revealing it on his deathbed.[31] Marx's wife left him twice but came back both times. Not that he cared. When she died, he didn't bother to attend her funeral.[32]

# Friedrich Engels

Friedrich Engels was also a study in contrasts, though perhaps not so much as Marx. He too, came from a wealthy background and lived in the lap of luxury while planning world revolution. A recent biography describes Engels as a sort-of revolutionary party animal. He enjoyed his drink and his motto was "take it easy." He was "proud of his lobster salad and liked to fox hunt. He hosted regular Sunday parties for London's left-wing intelligentsia and, as one regular put it, 'no one left before 2 or 3 in the morning.'"[33]

At the same time, he was ruthless and advocated wholesale violence. In 1849, Engels wrote, "The next world war will result in the disappearance from the face of the earth not only of reactionary classes and dynasties, but also of entire reactionary peoples. And that, too, is a step forward."[34]

Despite their similarities, one has to question Engels' sanity in forging a partnership with Marx. In addition to caring for Marx's illegitimate son, Engels supported Marx financially during their lifetime of collaboration. Marx was perpetually broke, though at least some of this could be blamed on his vanity and sexual appetites. According to Wheen:

> *Living in Dickensian poverty with bailiffs at his door, Marx wrote letters to Engels that were a 'ceaseless litany of wretchedness and woe.' Mostly, he scraped*

*by on handouts from his friend [Engels], who, having joined the Manchester branch of his father's firm, sent a 'regular consignment of small-denomination bank notes, pilfered from the petty cash box.' But Marx's dire straits... were due in no small part to his desire to keep up appearances. While Jenny [Marx's wife] ran about frantically trying to raise a couple of pounds to pay for a coffin for one of their children, her husband employed a loutish, libidinous and thoroughly useless private secretary merely because he thought it unseemly for a man of his position to be without one.*[35]

Whatever misgivings he may have had, however, Engels became Marx's partner in promoting communism, and was equally cognizant of its destructive force. In the *Communist Manifesto*, he wrote, "There are, besides, eternal truths, such as Freedom, Justice, etc., that are common to all states of society. But Communism abolishes eternal truths, it abolishes all religion and all morality, *instead of constituting them on a new basis; it therefore acts in contradiction to all past historical experience.*"[36] (Emphasis added.)

So how did they get away with this hypocrisy for 150 years? Have Marx's leftist followers simply been mesmerized by the phony aura about him built up over time as creator of the "infallible" doctrine of Marxism? Could he and Engels be, like everything else Marxist, immune to criticism simply because they are Marxists? Did their followers just ignore the knowledge of Marx's deep character flaws—available to anyone who researched him to any extent at all—because he had invented their beloved ideology? Were they ignorant of these facts, or was something else at work?

# Entrepreneurial Parasites

It turns out that Marx and Engels are personality types, and many prominent Communists reveal similar characteristics. Most were and are children of the wealthy, elitist classes, including Lenin, Mao and many others. While preaching Socialism their real goal is unbridled greed and power. I call them entrepreneurial parasites. They are amazing at using "revolution" to insert themselves in positions that allow them to leech society dry for their own benefit.

For example, as sons of a rich sugar plantation owner, the Castro brothers had it all. But it wasn't enough. At age 13, the defiant Fidel helped organize a sugar workers' strike against his own father's business.[37] Both brothers were thrown out of their first school and neither did well scholastically. They fell into the radical political scene at college. But for all their professed radicalism, taking over Cuba made them some of the wealthiest people in the world.

Fidel Castro, the humble revolutionary, began confiscating private property as soon as he took power. Forget baseball, communism was very good to him. Castro had amassed at least $900 million at his death in 2016.[38] Forbes estimated the Castro brothers' wealth could have been as much as 10 percent of Cuba's Gross Domestic Product.[39] But the Castro family own or control practically everything on the island. As Cuban expat and Castro expert Humberto Fontova states:

> *Castro can dispose of every business on his captive island in any manner he chooses. He can do the same with his every Cuban captive. He can just as easily rent them out as slave labor, as sell them for ransom, as jail them, as shoot them. Forbes' lists only the tiny tip of the Castro-wealth iceberg.[40]*

Even the great Cuban "revolution" was a myth. Few actually fought. One "battle" was won simply by broadcasting the sounds of gunfire and shouting over a shortwave radio. One of the biggest campaigns, the Battle of Santa Clara, was won by paying off the city military commander with a $100,000 note.[41] Despite the *New York Times* reporting "thousands dead" in a bloody civil war, total casualties, on both sides, during two years of "revolution" were 182.[42]

Raul Castro recently announced his retirement. The *Washington Post* noted that in so doing he "escapes accountability" for his and his brother's litany of crimes against the Cuban people.[43] The *Post* notes that Cuban leadership has been ceded "officially" to obscure government functionaries. "Unofficially," however, behind the scenes the Castro family remains firmly in charge of "economic and security matters..." The family keeps the money and the essential protection from the state. Nothing else really matters.

Note that for every single communist nation, leadership becomes either a multi-generational family dynasty, as in North Korea, Cuba and others, or a small cabal of leaders whose extended families enjoy unique privileges, as in China and Russia. The author detailed this years ago in a piece titled "Entrepreneurial Parasites."[44] Following Marx's example, this is what they all become, and many start off that way.

Bill Ayers, leader of the Weather Underground and mentor to Barack Obama, was the spoiled, rich son of Thomas Ayers, CEO of Consolidated Edison. Ayers and wife Bernardine Dohrn were supported by Ayers' father, Cuban intelligence and the North Vietnamese during their Weather Underground years.[45] When Ayers finally emerged from hiding, he said "Guilty as Hell, free as a bird-America is a great country!"[46] He and Bernardine were never convicted of their many crimes, likely including murder.

Ayers and Dohrn's adopted son, Chesa Boudin, advised the late Venezuelan dictator Hugo Chavez, and is now San Francisco District Attorney. In that role, he has led the charge for emptying prisons. Incredibly, Boudin claims doing so is "making San Francisco safer." He also cites a selfish reason. His father, David Gilbert, and mother, Kathie Boudin, were both domestic terrorist members of the May 19th Communist Organization. They participated in a 1981 Brinks armored car robbery that left three dead. Both were convicted of murder. Chesa claims it unfair that his father remains incarcerated.[47] Here is yet another example of this stunning entitlement mentality. Kathie was paroled in 2003 and now teaches at Columbia University. She was the role model for a 2012 play by David Mamet titled *The Anarchist*.[48]

Bill Ayers and many other 60s radicals idolize Mao Zedong. Some Obama administration officials did too, and we will no doubt find the same with Biden's crew.[49] The infamous Mao was responsible for as many as 80 million deaths during his bloody rule.[50] While his peasant background has always been emphasized, few know that his father was the wealthiest man in their rural community.

According to the biography, *Mao: the Unknown Story*, Mao was lazy, arrogant, insolent, and refused to work, despite his father's repeated attempts to find him suitable employment.[51] As a youth he was kicked out of four schools for being disobedient, at which point his father ceased supporting him financially. This meant he would have to work as a peasant. Horrified at the prospect, he was able to squirm out of it at age 14 by finding and marrying a girl four years older, a move his father approved. The money flowed again, but Mao cared nothing for his new wife. She died a year later.[52]

Mao went off to college and fell in with the country's leading Marxists. When the Soviet Comintern (Communist International) set up shop in China in 1920 Mao finally saw an opportunity for real advancement working for the Soviets.[53] During the Long March, when Mao's Communist forces walked 5,600 miles to avoid pursuing Nationalist troops, he and the other top Communists were kept safely away from danger and Mao rarely, if ever, walked. He was carried on a comfortable litter by porters, while he read "at his leisure."[54]

Black Lives Matter co-founder Patrisse Cullors calls herself a "trained Marxist." This turns out to be true, though not in the way she intended us to believe. With the recent revelation of her greedy misuse of millions of Black Lives Matter money for her own self-enrichment, it turns out that Patrisse Cullors is indeed a true Marxist. Under the mantle of "social justice" it appears she is just your run-of-the-mill grifter—but with a cover story.

Marxism appeals to those who grow up thinking they are special and by their very place, have nothing to prove. They already know it all. They are the kind of people attracted to simplistic, nihilistic, self-aggrandizing worldviews—it is an ideology that excuses all flaws in its adherents while concurrently ignoring or justifying their excesses.

In fact, the Soviets developed a profile for identifying the specific type of individual capable of leading a communist country—a certain personality type that would be attracted to the benefits and untroubled by the wall of deception, terrorism, torture and murder necessary to obtain them. The candidate had to be possessed of an unmatched viciousness, guile and feral cunning, while at the same time able to present a convincing public image of righteous belief in "the cause." These people are literally a class apart—a unique collection of monstrous sociopaths. The Soviets even carved out an exclusive caste for themselves by defining the rest of humanity out of it. We are all не наша (pronounced *nye nashe*), which means *not ours*, and they became adept at identifying those rare individuals possessing the qualities to become one of "ours."

Marx and Engels' violent exhortations informed the writings of subsequent leftist revolutionaries. While the justification is always "liberating the oppressed of the earth," or something along those lines, such insurrectionists betray a marked preoccupation with revenge and bloodlust. They envision a vaguely utopian future, but are people short on accomplishments and even shorter on the details of implementation. They focus virtually all of their efforts on destroying the current order. At this they become frighteningly adept.

# The Most Important Radical No One's Ever Heard Of

 One of the most important examples is anarchist Sergey Nechayev. Nechayev was also a member of the Russian Nihilist movement, the first movement to popularize the term "nihilism." The Nihilists became synonymous with political violence.[55] Nechayev penned a three-page pamphlet in 1869 titled *The Revolutionary Catechism*.[56] It was a blueprint for communist revolution that has since been further developed and used the world over by Communists everywhere.

A few quotes from Catechism capture the thrust of his intentions:

> *"The only form of revolution beneficial to the people is one which destroys the entire State to the roots and exterminates all the state traditions, institutions, and classes... "Our task is terrible, total, universal, and merciless destruction."*

Nechayev was only 22 years old when he wrote Catechism, having worked for a mere three years as a teacher at a St. Petersburg parish school. Yet he felt confident enough of his radical ideology to publish a manifesto calling for the extermination of the world.

This fantastic confluence of breathtaking conceit and stunning ignorance, coupled with a messianic determination to impose their own way on others, are the hallmarks of radicals from their earliest murmurings right up to today's standard bearers like Barack Obama, Hillary Clinton and a long list of Democrat politicians, from city councils to the White House. The administration of Joe Biden has shown itself to be the most radical yet, and while Biden himself may not be a Communist, he like many other prominent Democrats, owes his career to them. More about that later.

Nechayev's importance and contribution to radical politics cannot be overlooked. It was he who adopted the slogan, "The ends justify the means," as his own creed.[57] Sound familiar? That rationale has been the justification for every excessive "progressive" crusade ever since.

Nechayev was a true believer. He lived an austere life, even refusing release from jail when the cost to his compatriots would prevent a planned assassination attempt against Russian Czar Alexander II.[58] He remained in jail and the Czar was assassinated in 1881.

He also expected others to be just as committed. Taking a cue from Marx, Nechayev betrayed his followers to the police numerous times. But Marx probably did it to get paid. Nechayev's motive was ideological. He set up hundreds of other radicals by purposely sending them inflammatory propaganda, hoping they would be arrested and further radicalized by the experience. One of these, Vera Zasulich was imprisoned for four years because of Nechayev's machinations, and subsequently attempted to assassinate Fyodor Trepov, the Governor of St. Petersburg.[59]

Nechayev made an object lesson of one of his student followers, Ivan Ivanov, by murdering him in order to insure the commitment of his followers. As pretext he questionably accused Ivanov of being an informer.[60] While he escaped and lived free for 3 years before getting caught, 60 of his co-conspirators were immediately arrested.

Famed Russian novelist Fyodor Dostoevsky was alive in Nechayev's time and witnessed these events. They inspired Dostoevsky to drop everything he was doing and write *The Possessed* (aka *Demons* or *The Devils*) a searing mockery of the Catechism, Nechayev, and his circle of anarchist revolutionaries.[61]

*The Possessed* chillingly anticipated twentieth century Communist barbarity through the eyes of the character, Shigalov. In Shigalov's future, 90 percent of the world's population would become miserable slaves so the other 10 percent could enjoy freedom, and millions needed to die to create the new society. "Shigalovism," as it was called, has since been used as a derogatory term for Communist leadership styles.[62] Here is a quote from *The Possessed*:

> *He suggests a system of spying. Every member of the society spies on the others, and it's his duty to inform against them. Every one belongs to all and all to every one. All are slaves and equal in their slavery. In extreme cases he advocates slander and murder, but the great thing about it is equality. To begin with, the level of education, science, and talents is lowered. A high level of education and science is only possible for great intellects, and they are not wanted. The great intellects have always seized the power and been despots. Great intellects cannot help being despots and they've always done more harm than good. They will be banished or put to death. Cicero will have his tongue cut out, Copernicus will have his eyes put out, Shakespeare will be stoned—that's Shigalovism. Slaves are bound to be equal. There has never been either freedom or equality without despotism, but in the herd there is bound to be equality, and that's Shigalovism! Ha ha ha! Do you think it strange? I am for Shigalovism.*[63]

Dostoevsky was mocking Nechayev and his fellow nihilists' insane ideology. But doesn't this sound exactly like what is happening in our society today? Education is being reduced to its lowest common denominator, people are being urged to spy on their COVID noncompliant neighbors, banks and other creditors are considering social credit schemes like those already used in Communist China to enforce political conformity, and those who pose a threat to the established order are being censored, doxed, smeared, alienated from the community and often fired; rhetorically, if not literally, murdered.

## The Revolutionary Catechism

The little-known Catechism—also called *The Catechism of the Revolutionist*—is actually one of the major blueprints for the Left's strategies. As we shall see, it inspired Vladimir Lenin, the first leader of the USSR, and many others. And just as Saul Alinsky's *Rules for Radicals* was well known to leftists but virtually unknown to most normal people until recently, Nechayev's *Catechism* is must reading for radicals. In *Soul on Ice*, then Black Panther leader Eldridge Cleaver wrote of Nechayev:

> *I fell in love with Bakunin and Nechaev's [sic] Catechism of the Revolutionist—the principles of which, along with some of Machiavelli's advice, I sought to incorporate into my own behavior. I took the Catechism for my Bible.*[64]

Ironically, Cleaver was to have an epiphany later in life and became a Christian conservative supporter of Ronald Reagan—who he had once threatened to murder. He told people, "There *are* Communists under the bed."

Cleaver's Black Panthers clashed with the police frequently. When one of them was killed they accused the police of being the aggressors. He later said:

> *We went after the cops that night, but when we got caught, we said they came after us. We always did that. When you talk about the legacy of the '60's that's one legacy... [I]t helped to distort the image of*

*the police, but I've come to the point where I realize that our police department is necessary.*"[65] (Emphasis added.)

So, as we know, this strategy of vilifying police is nothing new, and Communism is its source. As stated in the article quoting Cleaver:

*This duplicitous strategy continues to the present day. "Protestors" still chant the "Hands up, don't shoot!" slogan from the Michael Brown shooting in Ferguson, Missouri even though the Obama-Holder Justice Department, after a thorough investigation and testimony from six black witnesses, cleared the police Officer. Truth is not of major concern to leftists when dictatorial control of a whole country is the goal.*[66]

The anarchist Mikhail Bakunin is sometimes cited as Catechism's co-author, but most, if not all, was written by Nechayev. While they had worked together, Bakunin distanced himself from Nechayev, largely because Nechayev was dishonest and generally untrustworthy. He officially broke with Nechayev in a letter written in 1870. But even then he acknowledged Nechayev's influence, saying, "[O]f all the Russian people whom I knew I considered you the most capable of carrying out this enterprise [the revolution] and I said to myself... that we were... unlikely to meet another man more dedicated and more able than you."[67]

Regarding the goals of their movement, however, Bakunin was completely on board. He wrote to Nechayev:

*The programme can be clearly expressed in a few words: total destruction of the framework of state and law and of the whole of the so-called bourgeois civilization by a spontaneous people's revolution invisibly led, not by an official dictatorship, but by a nameless and collective one, composed of those in favour of total people's liberation from all oppression, firmly united in a secret society and always and everywhere acting in support of a common aim and in accordance with a common programme.*[68]

Does that not sound like today's Antifa?

The Catechism is divided into four sections, I. Duties of the Revolutionary Toward Himself; II. The Relations of the Revolutionary toward his Comrades; III. The Relations of the Revolutionary toward Society, and IV. The Attitude of the [Revolutionary] Society toward the People. (The entire Catechism is reproduced in the Appendix.)

The most relevant point for us today is found in section IV, The Attitude of the Society toward the People. Here, Nechayev explains the method his revolutionaries will use to ignite the revolution:

*The Society [of revolutionary conspirators] has no aim other than the complete liberation and happiness of the masses—i.e., of the people who live by manual labor. Convinced that their emancipation and the achievement of this happiness can only come about as a result of an all-destroying popular revolt, <u>the Society will use all its resources and energy toward increasing and intensifying the evils and miseries of the people until at last their patience is exhausted and they are driven to a general uprising</u>.* (Emphasis added).

Read that section again. Nechayev spells out the revolutionary program in simple terms. All they want is our collective happiness. Sure. But in order to do that they must first destroy everything. To that end they will create such chaos, such animosity, such division and hatred, that *we will be the ones to initiate the revolution.*

23

Does that not sound like what is happening today? Everything the Left is doing in our streets, our schools, our universities, our media and our politics, is devoted to that one vicious objective: increasing our "evils and miseries," until we reach the breaking point. Then we will do the work for them. They will just have to clean up when it's over.

*It is a nonstop provocation campaign.* Just a few examples: releasing violent criminals from jail; dispensing with bond so they don't even bother showing up to court when arrested, or as has happened already, rearrested after release; not bothering to check illegal aliens swarming the border for COVID, while imposing harsh COVID restrictions on citizens; daily, nonstop lies and misinformation from the media; a Justice Department plainly politicized to go after President Trump, his allies and anyone else they deem a threat to the Left, while ignoring blatant criminality from the Left; treating January 6 as an "insurrection,"[69] while ignoring a years' worth of violence, death, theft and property damage committed by Antifa/BLM rioters. The contrast is simply stunning. The list is endless.

And make no mistake, if they didn't have the COVID excuse, it would be something else. Former President Obama ran a virtually nonstop provocation campaign against his political enemies, *i.e.,* patriotic Americans, during his entire tenure. It was President Obama who instigated the war against police that has since been played out to deadly effect, especially this past year. That was not a mistake. "Racial injustice" was the pretext; destabilizing our society was and is the real goal.

In Section III, The Relations of the Revolutionary toward Society, Nechayev lays out the Catechism's strategy for infiltrating and taking over society:

> *Aiming at implacable revolution, the revolutionary may and frequently must live within society while pretending to be completely different from what he really is, for he must penetrate everywhere, into all*

*the higher and middle-classes, into the houses of commerce, the churches, and the palaces of the aristocracy, and into the worlds of the bureaucracy and literature and the military...*

This important paragraph was the basis for the strategy outlined in Italian Communist Antonio Gramsci's Prison Notebooks. Gramsci advocated a "war of position" to establish power within the culture, and to do that, Communists needed to infiltrate and take over all of society's institutions. They have now done that. Over the past four years we have witnessed nameless bureaucrats working in federal, state and local bureaucracies working directly against elected leaders. This was frequently observed in the federal government under President Trump, where #RESIST became the prevalent attitude. Colleges and universities are another example, where speech codes, "safe spaces" and other insane "Woke" policies now dominate. Professors expressing any opposition are likely to be fired or at least harassed.

Further on, Catechism defines what "revolution" means:

*By a revolution, the Society does not mean an orderly revolt according to the classic western model—a revolt which always stops short of attacking the rights of property and the traditional social systems of so-called civilization and morality. Until now, such a revolution has always limited itself to the overthrow of one political form in order to replace it by another, thereby attempting to bring about a so-called revolutionary state. The only form of revolution beneficial to the people is one which destroys the entire State to the roots and exterminated all the state traditions, institutions, and classes...* (Emphasis added.)

In short, the idea is to destroy everything, root and branch. When you hear Antifa rioters shout "burn it all down," that is what they really mean.

In section I, Duties of the Revolutionary Toward Himself, Nechayev lays out the attitude revolutionaries should cultivate. Points 3 and 4 are key:

> *3. The revolutionist despises all doctrines and refuses to accept the mundane sciences, leaving them for future generations. He knows only one science: the science of destruction. For this reason, but only for this reason, he will study mechanics, physics, chemistry, and perhaps medicine. But all day and all night he studies the vital science of human beings, their characteristics and circumstances, at every possible level of social existence. The object is perpetually the same: the surest and quickest way of destroying the whole filthy order.*

> *4. The revolutionist despises public opinion. He despises and hates the existing social morality in all its manifestations. <u>For him, morality is everything which contributes to the triumph of the revolution. Anything that stands in its way is immoral and criminal.</u>* (Emphasis added.)

Point 4 explicitly rejects morality. If one has already rejected God, then that next step is easy. As frequently quoted from Dostoevsky's Brothers Karamazov, "without God… everything is permitted."[70]

But it goes further than that. Nechayev declares that anyone willing to stand up against the Left's insane agenda is a criminal by definition. That explains the otherwise incomprehensible logic of Antifa and BLM members attacking a pregnant black woman participating in a Trump rally and screaming "racist" or "Nazi" at her, or bludgeoning an elderly woman in a wheelchair. Anyone and everyone not explicitly and demonstrably on their side is the enemy, and is worthy, as Engels so kindly stated, of perishing "in the revolutionary world storm."[71]

Nechayev was a turbocharged version of Marx, even more determined to visit destruction on the world. His diabolical dreams would be fulfilled by future Communist leaders following the Catechism's blueprint.

## Targeted Chaos and Mass Murder

The "ends justifies the means" pretext is a license to use any and all methods, including mass murder, which Nechayev makes clear in the Catechism's third section. Here, it lays out the strategy and identifies those individuals within society that will require elimination, but divides them into groups whose longevity will depend exclusively on their temporary utility to the revolutionaries:

> *This filthy social order can be split up into several categories. The first category comprises those who must be condemned to death without delay. Comrades should compile a list of those to be condemned according to the relative gravity of their crimes; and the executions should be carried out according to the prepared order...*

The "crimes" he refers to are activities and people the revolutionaries don't like. In America, Trump supporters, unrepentant conservatives, tea party members, Christians, as well as many libertarians, would likely fall into this category. In fact, we've already seen it. The media and Democrat leaders repeatedly refer to President Trump as a "criminal," and treatment of some of his associates—like Roger Stone and Paul Manafort—is what you'd expect in a third world dictatorship. All Trump supporters are vilified as "conspiracy theorists," "extremists," "racists," "bigots,"

"Nazis," and even "domestic terrorists." The clear purpose is to marginalize and dehumanize their political enemies.

Democrats and leftists who put up any resistance fare no better. Lest you dismiss the Catechism as the rantings of a 150-year-old radical document, consider for a moment how the Left behaves publicly toward its enemies. Consider that, unlike Antifa/BLM rioters who have largely gotten a pass, participants in the January 6 protest, who were almost uniformly peaceful, are being arrested en masse, denied bail, and hounded to the ends of the earth.

But that is just the beginning. Late former undercover FBI informant Larry Grathwohl was the only informant to successfully penetrate the Weather Underground organization led by Obama friend and political mentor, Bill Ayers. Grathwohl was in the room when Ayers casually described how a post-revolutionary America would require the extermination of 25 million people. Grathwohl relates:

> *I bought up the subject of what's going to happen after we take over the government. We, we become responsible, then, for administrating, you know, 250 million people. And there were no answers. No one had given any thought to economics; how are you going to clothe and feed these people. The only thing that I could get was that they expected that the Cubans and the North Vietnamese and Chinese and the Russians would all want to occupy different portions of the United States.*

> *They also believed that their immediate responsibility would be to protect against what they called the counter-revolution. And they felt that this counter-revolution could best be guarded against by creating and establishing re-education centers in the southwest, where we would take all the people who needed to be re-educated into the new way of*

*thinking and teach them... how things were going to be.*

*I asked, well, what's going to happen to those people that we can't re-educate; that are die-hard capitalists. And the reply was that they'd have to be eliminated. And when I pursued this further, they estimated that they would have to eliminate 25 million people in these re-education centers. And when I say eliminate, I mean kill.*

*Twenty-five million people. I want you to imagine sitting in a room with 25 people, most of which have graduate degrees from Columbia and other well known educational centers, and hear them figuring out the logistics for the elimination of 25 million people. And they were dead serious.*[72]

Once again, the stunning arrogance and careless brutality of these people is shocking, and Bill Ayers launched the political career of Barack Obama in his living room after working closely with Obama and other radicals— including sharing office space—for years.[73]

Grathwohl's book on his Weather Underground experience, *Bringing Down America: An FBI Informer with the Weathermen*,[74] is an eye-opening exposé. This important work presents strong evidence that despite claims to the contrary by Ayers and Dohrn, the two were directly involved in the bombing murder of at least one person. Apologists for Ayers claim he has matured with age, but he and Dohrn have not renounced violence or ever apologized for what they did during the Weathermen years. They have slowed down with age, but their ideology is unchanged.

We continue with key points in Catechism's section III:

*The revolutionary enters the world of the State, of the privileged classes, of the so-called civilization, and he lives in this world only for the purpose of bringing about its speedy and total destruction. He is not a revolutionary if he has any sympathy for this world. He should not hesitate to destroy any position, any place, or any man in this world. He must hate everyone and everything in it with an equal hatred. All the worse for him if he has any relations with parents, friends, or lovers; he is no longer a revolutionary if he is swayed by these relationships.*

*When a list of those who are condemned is made and the order of execution is prepared, no private sense of outrage should be considered, nor is it necessary to pay attention to the hatred provoked by these people among the comrades or the people. Hatred and the sense of outrage may even be useful in so far as they incite the masses to revolt. It is necessary only to be guided by the relative usefulness of these executions for the sake of the revolution.* (Emphasis added.)

Nechayev points out here the utility of hatred. First, he insists the revolutionary must hate everyone. But the seemingly unjustifiable, irrational rage demonstrated by Antifa/BLM street rioters has a deadly logic. It purposely creates outrage among its targets in an effort to provoke a violent response. This is something few people outside of the Left understand about their seeming hatred for everything. It is *strategic hatred*, designed to inspire anger, fear, shame and self-doubt among its targets. *It is not real.* While low level followers may feel genuine animosity toward their victims, for the true revolutionary, hatred is a tool. To prove this, consider how this attitude vanishes instantly and the leftist becomes your best friend once you give in to his demands. *It is all for effect.*

Note what Nechayev says next:

*Above all, those who are especially inimical to the revolutionary organization must be destroyed; their violent and sudden deaths will produce the utmost panic in the government, depriving it of its will to action by removing the cleverest and most energetic supporters.*

The first people to be executed are always those expected to be the most trouble. Today, that would be Conservatives and Trump supporters. Hillary Clinton called them a "basket of deplorables." The constant vilification of communism's opponents is all designed to dehumanize their enemies, starting with the ones who they know will not go down without a fight.

*The second group comprises those who will be spared for the time being in order that, by a series of monstrous acts, they may drive the people into inevitable revolt.*

Here Nechayev is talking about people like the Antifa/BLM rioters themselves! They consider themselves the tip of the revolutionary spear. And they are. But once the true leaders are secure in power, these lunatics will have outlived their usefulness and be exterminated. Same with many of the radical activist groups. They will be shocked to find themselves swept up. We all agree they are an insufferable pain in the neck—but that is their function right now. Once the revolution is won, the leaders will waste no time dispatching these whiny, self-righteous, demanding asses.

Those violent criminals now being let out of jail are another example. Some of those released have committed murder already. In just one example, an Oklahoma man given early release as part of a mass commutation committed 3 murders, which included cutting a neighbor's heart out.[75] And California recently announced that 76,000 more criminals, including over 63,000 violent felons, have now been scheduled for early release.[76] Illegal aliens given free rein in America have also committed numerous gruesome crimes way out of proportion to their numbers in the population. It creates absolute outrage among most Americans and legal immigrants, and that of course is the intention: "increasing the evils and miseries of the people until at last their patience is exhausted..."

> *The third category consists of a great many brutes in high positions, distinguished neither by their cleverness nor their energy, while enjoying riches, influence, power, and high positions by virtue of their rank. These must be exploited in every possible way; they must be implicated and embroiled in our affairs, their dirty secrets must be ferreted out, and they must be transformed into slaves. Their power, influence, and connections, their wealth and their energy, will form an inexhaustible treasure and a precious help in all our undertakings.*

> *The fourth category comprises ambitious office-holders and liberals of various shades of opinion. The revolutionary must pretend to collaborate with them, blindly following them, while at the same time, prying out their secrets until they are completely in his power. They must be so compromised that there is no way out for them, and then they can be used to create disorder in the State.* (Emphases added.)

We can immediately think of whole lists of people who fall into these categories: most Democrat members of Congress, and sadly, some Republicans as well. Certainly Joe Biden, Kamala Harris, Nancy Pelosi (D-CA), Eric Swalwell (D-CA), Chuck Schumer (D-NY), Jerry Nadler (D-NY), perhaps GOP Minority Leader Mitch McConnell, (R-KY), and many others.

Convicted pedophile Jeffrey Epstein put many well-known influencers in compromising positions. This activity and the laundry list of influential people who knew Epstein or traveled on his "Lolita Express," could fill a book. In fact, it did—his little black book. Was he recruited to do this? We will never know. He suffered what appeared to be an "assisted" suicide in prison.[77]

> *The fifth category consists of those doctrinaires, conspirators, and revolutionists who cut a great figure on paper or in their cliques. They must be constantly driven on to make compromising declarations: as a result, the majority of them will be destroyed, while a minority will become genuine revolutionaries.*

Hillary Clinton and many top Democrats fit in this category. They talk a good game but it is all academic. They live in comfortable affluence and leave the dirty work to others. They willingly collaborate with our enemies. Bill Clinton did. Hillary did. Joe Biden and many members of Congress have. Will a Communist government led by Russia or China let them live? Why would they? Share the wealth? Are you kidding?

Nechayev further stratifies the list of eventual victims in further points, identifying more classes of people who can prove useful to the revolution before their extermination. A number of U.S. politicians, pundits and industrialists likely fall into one or more of these categories.

One that immediately comes to mind is George Soros, sugar daddy to the Left. While he presents himself as a savvy hedge fund operator, some, if not all, of his ill-gotten gains are the result of illegal forms of stock market transactions. This modern-day robber baron was convicted of insider trading in France and fined for market manipulation in Hungary.[78]

Known as the man who "broke the Bank of England," he has manipulated the currencies of numerous countries. He is despised in Britain, France, Belgium, his home country of Hungary, Thailand, Indonesia and elsewhere for the wreckage he has caused.[79] Meanwhile, in the U.S. he applies his financial market plunder to practically every destructive leftist initiative there is. His latest has been to support prosecutors like Chesa Boudin, who not only empty prisons and abandon bail, but actually refuse to prosecute crimes. Yet despite Soros's obviously subversive efforts, he walks free without consequence because one political party is beholden to him.

It is essential to reiterate here that Nechayev describes entire categories of people who are preordained to die—the sentence of death being postponed only so long as they are useful to the revolution. The Catechism lays it out in black and white.

The Catechism concludes on this chilling note: *To weld this world into one single unconquerable and all-destructive force—this is our organization, our conspiracy, our task.*

Nechayev's blueprint for wholesale extermination became formalized with the Red Terror, the Soviet Union's official campaign of arbitrary arrest, disappearances, torture, and mass murder initiated in 1918. There was even a newspaper named *Red Terror*. Ukrainian KGB Chief Martin Latsis outlined the Terror's goals:

> *We are not fighting against single individuals. We are exterminating the bourgeoisie as a class. Do not look in materials you have gathered for evidence that a suspect acted or spoke against the Soviet authorities. The first question you should ask him is what class he belongs to, what is his origin, education, profession. These questions should determine his fate. This is the essence of the Red Terror.*[80]

Soviet Comintern (Communist International) leader Grigory Zinoviev explained:

*To overcome our enemies we must have our own socialist militarism. We must carry along with us 90 million out of the 100 million of Soviet Russia's population. As for the rest, we have nothing to say to them. They must be annihilated.*[81]

Both Latsis and Zinoviev were later executed by Stalin. Apparently, they had outlived their usefulness too.

## State-Sponsored Genocide

The Catechism's prescriptions have found their most gruesome application in Communist genocides the world over. It is an unmatched record of barbarity, responsible for more deaths during times of peace than in all the wars of history combined. Here is a partial list of communism's victims over the past century:[82]

> Soviet Union, 20 million;
> Communist China, 65 million;
> Nazi Germany, 6 million;
> Vietnam, 3.8 million dead (including a minimum estimated 250,000 boat people who perished trying to escape);[83]
> Cambodia, 2 million; (note that Cambodia's total population was only 7 million.)
> North Korea, 2 million;
> Afghanistan, 1.5 million;
> Africa, 1.7 million;
> Eastern Europe, 1 million;
> Latin America, 150,000;
> Iraq under Saddam, 190,000;[84]
> Cuba, between 35,000 and 141,000.[85]

Some will argue that these mass executions are the fault of brutal leaders, not the system itself. Westerners tend to personalize these objectionable characteristics. Thus, we denounce Stalin the villain, Hitler the butcher, Saddam and his "henchmen." Many see the leader as an aberration, rather than a product of the system. But the reverse is true.

By its very nature the Communist model requires leaders like Lenin, Stalin, Castro, Assad, Mao and Pol Pot—all clever, devious, diabolical, mass murderers. The monstrous political sewer created by the Communist system spawns only those gruesome enough to swim in it. Meanwhile, the economic system they impose causes extreme hardship. Communists know they will face violent opposition so they simply evaluate those among the various classes likely to cause problems and kill them preemptively. This wave of mass genocide does not occur because of madmen's excesses. Premeditated murder of 5 - 20 percent of the population is Communist doctrine, and Nechayev was its inspiration.[86]

Marx and Engels' views on political violence were alleged to have moderated in later years, yet their followers must not have gotten the memo. Over and above grinding poverty for the masses and a rapacious foreign policy, genocidal mass murder is Marxism's greatest lasting legacy.[87]

While the history of communist genocide is well-known, it may seem a stretch to impute such impulses to today's Left. But is it? Sure, you say, Bill Ayers and his Weather Underground discussed exterminating 25 million people, but that was just one small group of very extreme radicals having a bull session. Besides, now he has grown up and become a supposedly respected college professor. He is indeed "respected" but only by other radicals who also grew up and weaseled their way into the educational establishment. However, he has never renounced violence, even as recently as 2014.[88] A New York Times interview with Ayers was published on September 11, 2001. In it he said, "EVERYTHING was absolutely ideal on the day I bombed the Pentagon... "I don't regret setting bombs...I feel we didn't do enough."[89] His odious wife, Bernardine Dohrn, has been even more blatant.

But American radical leftists are not yet fully in charge. They remain somewhat constrained by what remains of our crumbling political system and rule-of-law. But their rhetoric is little different from radicals of the past, and even within the constraints of our system, they engage in tactics that can only be described as savage. At the drop of a hat, they seek to destroy the lives of anyone who stands in their way using a blizzard of defamation, threats, lawsuits and boycotts. As President, Obama used the power of the federal government, notably but not exclusively, the IRS, the EPA and the Bureau of Land Management to target Americans.

The Biden administration has picked up the pace. In addition to using the FBI to target anyone at the Capitol during the January 6 "insurrection," the administration has now targeted for removal any and all Republicans serving in the U.S. military. Finally, the administration, Congressional Democrats, their media, big tech, education and Hollywood allies relentlessly vilify the entire population of Trump-supporting Americans. Ask yourself: given unbridled power, would today's Left be any nicer to its opponents than Stalin's secret police?

Nechayev lays out the Left's game plan in brutally honest terms. Leftists will vigorously deny this, but then they rarely tell the truth. Even amongst themselves, they speak in code words and vague references, lest the reality of their intentions become well known. The Catechism methodology has even been awarded its own title in leftist terminology. It is called "Catastrophism" and the Left is intimately familiar with it.

Not all are enamored. Some Marxist intellectuals, for example Eduard Bernstein, eschewed catastrophism as a methodology for creating socialist society. He wrote:

> *In all advanced countries we see the privileges of the capitalist bourgeoisie yielding step by step to*

*democratic organisations. Under the influence of this, and driven by the movement of the working classes which is daily becoming stronger, a social reaction has set in against the exploiting tendencies of capital, a counteraction which, although it still proceeds timidly and feebly, yet does exist, and is always drawing more departments of economic life under its influence. Factory legislation, the democratising of local government, and the extension of its area of work, the freeing of trade unions and systems of co-operative trading from legal restrictions, the consideration of standard conditions of labour in the work undertaken by public authorities—all these characterise this phase of the evolution.*

*But the more the political organisations of modern nations are democratised the more the needs and opportunities of great political catastrophes are diminished. He who holds firmly to the catastrophic theory of evolution must, with all his power, withstand and hinder the evolution described above, which, indeed, the logical defenders of that theory formerly did. But is the conquest of political power by the proletariat simply to be by a political catastrophe? Is it to be the appropriation and utilisation of the power of the State by the proletariat exclusively against the whole non-proletarian world?* "[90]

In the last sentence, Bernstein betrayed a bit of worry and conscience. In a post-revolutionary world, he would likely be quickly added to one of Nechayev's extermination lists. Among a crowd where the true goal is power, the thugs will always win out over the theoreticians. This is indeed what has happened. True leftists seek raw power and care little for the timid sensitivities of socialists like Bernstein.

The late John P. Roche, counselor to both Presidents JFK and Lyndon Johnson, was a small "d" democratic socialist and co-founder of Americans for Democratic Action. When he announced his support for the Vietnam War, he was banished by his fellow leftists. He explained the reality of Communism this way:

> *Most analyses of Marxism-Leninism are philosophical exercises conducted in the intellectual stratosphere. This approach has a limited utility, but is based on a deeply flawed premise: that Marxism-Leninism is a form of high theory, rather than an operational code for a new-style mafia, far more interested in finding a rationale for seizing or wielding power than in liberating 'prisoners of starvation' or the 'wretched of the earth.*[91]

# Vladimir Lenin and the Strategy of Hate

Vladimir Ilyich Lenin (aka Vladimir Ilyich Ulyanov), was the leader of the Bolshevik coup that overthrew the Russian government in October 1917. The hyped "October Revolution" was accomplished in two days with minimal force and only two casualties. Although it was of great political importance to the Soviets, it was such a non-event that they had to film a reenactment in 1920 for propaganda purposes, showing thousands storming the Czar's Winter Palace to win a rousing victory for the proletariat.[92]

Lenin greatly admired Nechayev and enthusiastically embraced his call for mass murder.[93] As early as 1906, well before the Soviet takeover in Russia, Lenin wrote, "We would be deceiving both ourselves and the people if we concealed from the masses the necessity of a desperate, bloody war of extermination, as the immediate task of the coming revolutionary action."[94]

Of Nechayev he later wrote: "We must publish all of Nechayev's works. He must be researched and studied. We must find all his writings, decode his pseudonyms, collect it all and print it."[95]

In fact, Nechayev may have indirectly provoked Lenin's final radicalization. Czar Alexander II was assassinated by Nechayev's co-conspirators in 1881. Six years later Lenin's older brother, Alexander Ulyanov, and 14 co-conspirators sought to murder Czar Alexander III on the anniversary of his father's assassination. The plot failed, and Ulyanov was caught and subsequently hanged with four others. According to at least one account, this had a heavy influence on Lenin's psychology.[96]

Speaking of psychology, Lenin is yet another personification of the Marxist personality type. He has been described as, "Self-righteous, rude, demanding, ruthless, despotic, formalistic, bureaucratic, disciplined, cunning, intolerant, stubborn, one-sided, suspicious, distant, asocial, cold-blooded, ambitious, purposive, vindictive, spiteful, a grudge-holder, and a coward... Lenin appeared to be unpretentious and soft-spoken. His enormous willpower was hidden behind a facade of modesty. His personality was basically cold, yet he gave the impression of warmth."[97]

Does this not sound familiar? Communism, or maybe we should call it "progressive" despotism, should be defined and treated as a psychological disorder.

In Catechism, Nechayev insisted his followers create hardship, sow chaos and hate, "*increasing and intensifying the evils and miseries of the people...*"

Lenin was the first to articulate this as a practical strategy. He said, "We must be ready to employ trickery, deceit, law-breaking, withholding and concealing truth ...We can and must write in a language which sows among the masses hate, revulsion, and scorn toward those who disagree with us." [98]

In the Soviet Union, and any other Communist nation for that matter, individuals so vilified could face a death sentence.[99] But the tactic was urged on party members worldwide as suggested by this 1943 message from the Soviet Communist Party to the Communist parties of the world:

> *Members and front organizations must continually embarrass, discredit and degrade our critics. When obstructionists become too irritating, label them as fascist or Nazi or anti-Semitic... constantly associate those who oppose us with those names that already*

*have a bad smell. The association will, after enough repetition, become 'fact' in the public mind.*[100]

Lenin and his Bolsheviks also believed that stifling speech was essential to their cause. He said:

*Why should freedom of speech and freedom of the press be allowed? Why should a government which is doing what it believes is right allow itself to be criticized? It would not allow opposition by lethal weapons. Ideas are much more fatal things than guns.*[101]

So now you know where it all comes from. Today you can see the "hate" tactic in operation every day when left-wing professors, journalists, performers and politicians ridicule, misrepresent, threaten or just suppress statements by anyone with an opposing view, or facts that might upset the leftist narrative. The Southern Poverty Law Center, Media Matters for America, the ACLU and even the Anti-Defamation League are assisting in this effort today. Social media does the same by "deplatforming," "shadow-banning," and other forms of censorship, while online payment processors discriminate against those with a politically incorrect mission or message, financially crippling them.

It is an unscrupulous, mean-spirited, self-serving and dangerous form of psychological terrorism that is putting our nation at war with itself. It has reduced our political discourse to infantile, elementary school name-calling. It is a national disgrace, delivered to us entirely from the Left. But they do it because it is so easy to do—remember, most leftists are lazy, arrogant, ignorant fools who could not defend their beliefs if their lives depended on it—and because it is very effective at marginalizing opponents; the target can lose friends, jobs, access to major communications platforms and standing in the community. It is a form of political warfare. So next time someone calls you "Nazi," "bigot," "xenophobe" or whatever, they are just parroting Lenin, though many are too ignorant to know it. Don't get upset or try to defend yourself. It's pointless. Just say: "Ah! So, you must be a Leninist!"

# Strategic Corruption & Cultural Terrorism

Whenever the Left comes up with a new proclamation or policy, we tend to take it seriously, considering each one afresh as if it were some novel proposition on the laws of physics. But upon closer examination, we realize it is simply a repackaged version of the same old ideas first embraced by Marx—and even those weren't new. Whether it is abortion, environment, gun control, taxes, welfare, women's rights, gay rights, minority rights, illegal immigration, global warming or something else, the issue is never the issue. It merely serves as a vehicle to upend our culture and divide America into warring fragments, each time allowing the Left to step in as conquering hero. This is not an opinion, but the stated objective of socialists going all the way back to the man who calls himself the founder of communism, Karl Marx.

But Marx was wrong about almost everything. The revolution didn't't turn out anything like he expected. The masses were not driven to revolt in Germany, Britain, or anywhere else. In Russia, a confluence of unique circumstances aggravated by a costly and incompetently executed war against the Germans during World War I, and compounded by the missteps of the nascent and weak Socialist government of Alexander Kerensky, allowed the Bolsheviks—intent on seizing power by any means—to take over Russia.

Nobody in the West seemed inclined to participate in a bloody uprising. The Communists recognized that converting the West, especially America, wouldn't't be easy. Our strong Christian tradition was anathema to the communist idea. We had a strong military and our market-based economic system did not appear to be sowing the seeds of its own destruction, as Marx's theory predicted. Instead, it grew in leaps and bounds, bringing the West, and the U.S. in particular, into a period of unprecedented material wealth.

But Marxists are nothing if not flexible. Doctrinaire Marxism would have to make a tactical retreat. According to the Left, Marx's theories were beyond reproach; they just needed a little help from time to time. If our proletariat could not be roused into blazing revolution, they would have to be lured into it.

Our constitutional republic requires an attentive, involved, educated, and ethical electorate. A distracted, self-absorbed, unprincipled electorate—even if highly educated—is susceptible to charlatans of all varieties. Note that being credentialed with an undergraduate or even graduate degree these days does not necessarily make the holder "educated." Indeed, American university graduates are increasingly *uneducated* regarding our heritage, culture, republican form of government and a host of other things. This did not happen by mistake.

We all have primordial lusts and are all vulnerable to them. They have often been referred to as the seven deadly sins: pride, greed, anger, envy, lust, gluttony and sloth. They are simply manifestations of our basic survival instincts for present security (physical sustenance, shelter, and protection from external dangers) and future security (financial wealth, social station, and procreation) taken to excess. When given free rein they become toxic. The desire for safety and security grows into insatiable greed for money, power and envy toward others. The procreative instinct becomes promiscuity or worse.

Taken to the extreme, satisfying these instincts can turn into obsession, creating morally corrupt, willful, selfish, untrustworthy, and sometimes dangerous people. Such people create turmoil and conflict. Applied to an entire society, it is a prescription for corruption, animosity, alienation, degeneracy, and chaos. A nation thus compromised becomes so oblivious and self-absorbed it does not bother to consider—or even recognize—looming threats.

Communists have always known this. Early on they began developing the philosophies, tactics, and institutions to inject poisonous ideas into our society that would capitalize on those natural human tendencies. Lenin and his associates initiated covert "influence" operations against the West, and ultimately at America, the Main Enemy, using the transmission belts of culture: media, Hollywood, the arts and academia, to push Soviet propaganda and undermine Western civilization. Some of the most important tacticians in this enterprise were Willi Münzenberg, Georgi Lukacs and Antonio Gramsci.

## Willi Münzenberg

Willi Münzenberg was a Communist agent of the Soviet-sponsored Comintern. Like Nechayev, most Americans have never heard of him. Yet he was one of the most influential agents of influence the Soviets ever had. Münzenberg was a dedicated Communist from an early age and in his teens was already adept at subversive activities including money laundering, document forgery and cross-border smuggling.[102] Leon Trotsky spotted the then-26-year-old Münzenberg in 1914, and immediately recognized talent. Trotsky introduced him to Lenin and he was part of Lenin's inner circle from then on.

Münzenberg was an indefatigable true believer and an organizational genius who set up thousands of Communist front organizations in Germany, France, and the U.S. during the 1920s and 1930s. Quoting from the UK's *Times Higher Education*, "At its height his empire comprised at least two daily newspapers, one weekly and countless magazines; the total circulation ran to many millions. Münzenberg controlled film distributors and theatre companies. Some of the most famous names of European literature … were at his beck and call…"[103] In his treatise on Münzenberg, *Double Lives*, author Stephen Koch writes:

> *The writers, artists, journalists, scientists, educators, clerics, columnists, film-makers, and publishers, either under his influence or regularly manipulated by his "Münzenberg men," present a startling list of notables from that era, from Ernest Hemingway to John Dos Passos to Lillian Hellman to Georg Grosz to Irwin Piscator to André Malraux to Andrée Gide to Bertolt Brecht to Dorothy Parker … to Kim Philby, Guy Burgess, and Anthony Blunt. Indeed, the entire cultural and intellectual apparatus of "idealistic" Stalinism outside Russia, and much of its secret apparat, operated within a system Münzenberg had guided into place…*[104]

Münzenberg articulated his plan in Comintern meetings held in the Soviet Union during the early years of Soviet rule:

> *Münzenberg clearly understood that the Revolution required something more than winning over "the masses." Speaking to a Comintern packed with intellectuals, he pounded at his point: "We must organize the intellectuals." The revolution needed middle-class opinion makers—artists, journalists, "people of good will," novelists, actors, playwrights*

*... humanists, people whose innocent sensitivities weren't yet cauterized to nervelessness by the genuine white-hot radical steel.*

*Lenin recoiled at this idea ... Here were the people he loathed most—he who loathed so many people. Middle-class do-gooders? Bourgeois intellectuals clutching their precious "freedom of conscience"? Lenin would kill and imprison them by the thousands. It took him a while—until 1921—to consent to use them too.*

Lenin never abandoned his contempt for these "intellectuals," calling them "simpletons." But the term of use most commonly attributed to Lenin is "useful idiots." He did not coin the phrase "useful idiots" even though it is widely credited to him. But it has become popularized as the term of use for those Western fools who enthusiastically embrace the "revolution," blissfully unaware that they are marked for extinction in Catechism's order of execution once they've outlived their usefulness. Münzenberg also saw collaboration as a useful way to hide the Communists' true goals:

*"We must avoid being a purely communist organization," Münzenberg explained to his men. "We must bring in other names, other groups, to make persecution more difficult." Middle-class opinion makers, liberal sympathizers, however much echt [genuine] Bolsheviks despised them, must be used. Co-option may have struck hardline Leninists as soft, but as Münzenberg pointed out, the powder keg was not blowing, despite all kinds of sparks...[105]*

Once again, we hear echoes of Nechayev's Catechism in Münzenberg's words, "*The revolutionary must pretend to collaborate with them, blindly following them, while at the same time, prying out their secrets until they are completely in his power... and then they can be used to create disorder in the State."*

But Münzenberg's greatest contribution was to articulate a strategy that would use the intelligentsia to corrupt Western culture. He said:

> *We must organize the intellectuals and use them to make Western civilization stink. Only then, after they have corrupted all its values and made life base, can we impose the Dictatorship of the Proletariat.*[106]

## Georgi Lukacs

Münzenberg was aided in this project by Georgi Lukacs, who during Béla Kun's short-lived Hungarian Soviet Republic (March to August 1919), served as People's Commissar for Culture and Education. Reflecting the destructive impulses and towering arrogance of his intellectual forebears, Lukacs proclaimed, "I saw the revolutionary destruction of society as the one and only solution to the cultural contradictions of the epoch ... Such a worldwide overturning of values cannot take place without the annihilation of the old values and the creation of new ones by the revolutionaries."[107]

Lukacs pioneered the attack on Western culture by using sex as a weapon of moral corruption. He instituted a radical program of mandated sex education in schools which provided explicit, illustrated, "how-to" instruction to children while exhorting them to reject Christian morality.[108]

This was accompanied by a campaign of vilification against Christianity and Christian traditions, very much like what is happening today in America. There was also a marketing campaign for adult women, exhorting them to abandon traditional values and marriage in favor of sexual licentiousness.

Lukacs called his program *"Cultural Terrorism,"* and it infuriated Hungary's Catholic population.[109] Following World War I both Czechoslovakia and Romania attempted to overthrow Hungary. Béla Kun's Communists were able to repel the Czech troops but large segments of the population and the military would not fight when they realized the Communists' true objectives. Béla Kun was forced to flee to the Soviet Union in August following a Romanian offensive and his government collapsed.

## Antonio Gramsci

 Antonio Gramsci, a prominent Italian Communist in the 1920s, spent the bulk of 1922 and 1923 in the Soviet Union and attended the 4th Comintern Congress, where he was exposed to Münzenberg. In 1924 he became the leader of Italy's Communist Party. Jailed by Mussolini in 1926, he further developed Nechayev's and Münzenberg's ideas in what came to be known as the *Prison Notebooks*.

Gramsci never left prison and died there in 1937. But his Notebooks survived him, and were picked up with enthusiasm by American Marxists, most notably, 60s radicals. According to Gramsci, capitalism's power or "hegemony" rested in its institutions, that is, churches, schools, the media, Hollywood, the military government and political parties.

The answer of course was to infiltrate, subvert, dominate and control these institutions to serve Communist ends. He advocated doing this not through revolution or warfare, but rather by a "war of position" in the culture. Communist subversives would seed socialist ideas gradually by penetrating the various institutions of culture until those ideas took hold and were accepted as mainstream. Eventually the concepts would become embedded in public policy. This has come to be known as "the long march through the institutions."

The original idea, as you now know from reading this book, came from Nechayev's Catechism, when he said:

> *Aiming at implacable revolution, the revolutionary may and frequently must live within society while pretending to be completely different from what he really is, for he must penetrate everywhere, into all the higher and middle-classes, into the houses of commerce, the churches, and the palaces of the aristocracy, and into the worlds of the bureaucracy and literature and the military…*

Like Marx and many other Communists, Gramsci loved to hear himself talk, using his 3,000-page *Prison Notebooks* to articulate a strategy described by Nechayev in one paragraph.

Münzenberg identified those who would carry out this strategy as the "intellectuals." One of the most widely acclaimed modern "intellectuals" was Joseph Buttigieg, father to failed presidential candidate and now Secretary of Transportation, Pete Buttigieg. Joseph was a prominent Marxist and Notre Dame professor who was well known in leftist circles as a leading scholar of Gramsci.[110] He co-founded and presided over the International Gramsci Society and translated all of Gramsci's work in a project that took him three decades before its initial 1992 publication.[111] He personified Münzenberg's call to *"organize the intellectuals and use them to make Western civilization stink,"* a perfect example of Lenin's "useful idiots." Pete Buttigieg proudly carries on his father's tradition.

# The Frankfurt School

In 1923, Lukacs attended a "Marxist Study Week" in Frankfurt, Germany organized by Herman Weil, yet another spoiled, rich son of a wealthy German industrialist. Lukacs was so well received that Weil decided to fund a new university in Frankfurt that would further develop Lukacs and Münzenberg's, ideas. They called it the bland title, "School of Social Research" to hide its malevolent Communist mission. It became known as the Frankfurt School.

With Hitler's rise to power in 1933, the Frankfurt School Communists faced a serious dilemma. Most were also Jewish, so they had two marks against them. Ironically, almost all of these scholars were, like Marx, virulent anti-Semites, despite their Jewish heritage. They fled Germany to England, France and America assisted by Edward R. Murrow, who managed the Emergency Committee in Aid of Displaced Foreign Scholars, a program of the Institute for International Education that resettled educators facing Nazi repression.[112] Morrow would later become a famous CBS newscaster.

Not coincidentally, Senator Joseph McCarthy later accused Murrow of being a possible Communist. While at IIE, Murrow had organized summer training sessions in Moscow for two years in a row, and had a close friendship with Laurence Duggan, a suspected Soviet agent. Laurence was the son of IIE Director Stephen Duggan. In the 1990s it was confirmed that Laurence had been working for the Soviets.[113]

Murrow was a protégé of John Dewey, the "progressive" so-called father of public education. Dewey had also visited the Soviet Union, where his books were used to implement the Soviet education system.[114] Dewey's *Democracy and Education* became the bible for Columbia University's Teachers College, where Dewey taught, and is used in schools of education throughout the U.S. Dewey toured the USSR in 1928 and subsequently urged President Roosevelt to grant the Soviets diplomatic recognition.[115]

The Frankfurt School was reinstituted at Columbia University's Teachers College with Dewey's help. Dewey also founded the New School for Social Research in New York City, where some of the Frankfurt School Communists settled. To this day, the school brags of its Frankfurt School heritage.

## Critical Theory

In 1843, well before he wrote the *Communist Manifesto*, Marx stated "The proclamation of ready-made solutions for all time is not our affair..." This directly contradicts his professed goals stated in the *Communist Manifesto* to save the "workers of the world." But Marx was more honest here. He concluded that "...we realize all the more fully what we have to accomplish in the present. I am talking about a ruthless criticism of everything existing."[116] His true goal was to attack every aspect of Western culture. He added, "The criticism must not be afraid of its own conclusions, nor of conflict with the powers that be."[117]

Once established in the U.S. Frankfurt School communists took Marx's cue and proceeded to do just that. Borrowing heavily from Lukacs' vision of cultural terrorism, in 1937, leading Frankfurt School scholar Max Horkheimer published an essay titled "Traditional and Critical Theory." It described a new school of thought aimed at "critiquing and changing society as a whole."[118] Echoing the Soviets and especially Lenin's call to *"write in a language that inspires hate, revulsion and scorn toward those who disagree with us,"* Frankfurt School teaching relentlessly accused Western societies of being "the world's greatest repositories of racism, sexism, xenophobia, homophobia, anti-Semitism, fascism, and Nazism."[119] Sound familiar?

Critical Theory attacks Christianity, capitalism, authority, the family, patriarchy, hierarchy, morality, tradition, sexual restraint, loyalty, patriotism, and nationalism—any and all foundations of society, in order to destroy the culture and "make Western civilization stink."[120] In a *Catholic Insight* magazine article, author Timothy Matthews listed the Frankfurt School's key goals for Western society that grew out of Critical Theory:[121]

1.  The creation of racism offenses
2.  Continual change to create confusion
3.  The teaching of sex and homosexuality to children
4.  The undermining of schools' and teachers' authority
5.  Huge immigration to destroy identity
6.  The promotion of excessive drinking
7.  Emptying of churches
8.  An unreliable legal system with bias against victims of crime
9.  Dependency on the state or state benefits
10. Control and dumbing down of media
11. Encouraging the breakdown of the family

Critical Theory has come to be known as Cultural Marxism or Political Correctness. Interestingly, the term "politically correct" also comes from the Communists themselves. It was a derogatory term coined in the 1950s to describe Communists who slavishly followed the Party line.[122] If you didn't, you weren't politically correct. Apparently, today we are all toeing the Party line. Theodore Dalyrmple offers a very insightful observation on political correctness:

> *Political correctness is Communist propaganda writ small. In my study of Communist societies, I came to the conclusion that the purpose of Communist*

*propaganda was not to persuade or convince, nor to inform, but to humiliate; and therefore, the less it corresponded to reality the better. When people are forced to remain silent when they are being told the most obvious lies, or even worse when they are forced to repeat the lies themselves, they lose once and for all their sense of probity. To assent to obvious lies is to co-operate with evil, and in some small way to become evil oneself. One's standing to resist anything is thus eroded, and even destroyed. A society of emasculated liars is easy to control. I think if you examine political correctness, it has the same effect and is intended to.*[123]

Writing in American Thinker, Linda Kimball summarized Frankfurt School objectives:

*The primary goal of the Frankfurt School was to translate Marxism from economic terms into cultural terms. It would provide the ideas on which to base a new political theory of revolution based on culture, harnessing new oppressed groups for the faithless proletariat. Smashing religion, morals, it would also build a constituency among academics, who could build careers studying and writing about the new oppression.*[124]

These are all widely recognizable, alarming trends in our society, which we assume are unrelated, unintended consequences of choices our society has made. In a certain sense this is true, because we have made most of these choices ourselves. But behind it all was a deliberate strategy to sabotage our moral compass, weaponize our instincts, and turn our culture inside out. In the background we hear Nechayev once again exhorting the revolutionary "society" to *"use all its resources and energy toward increasing and intensifying the evils and miseries of the people until at last their patience is exhausted and they are driven to a general uprising."*

## The Authoritarian Personality

Another contribution of the Frankfurt School was a book published in 1950 called *The Authoritarian Personality*, co-authored by Theodor Adorno and three other Frankfurt School scholars. It created an "F" scale (F for Fascist) that, using bogus surveys rigged to provide the answers they wanted, found that any person who subscribes to the U.S. Constitution, the rule of law, capitalism and any other Western beliefs, is automatically branded fascist, racist, bigot, etc., even if he or she doesn't know it.

This reading found its way, like so much else pushed by the Frankfurt School Communists, into the mainstream of intellectual discourse.[125] So you and I, as patriotic, open-minded Americans of whatever color creed or ethnicity, are automatically branded "fascists."

More and more, we hear the suggestion that Trump supporters, patriots and conservatives generally are mentally ill—a claim based on the bogus *Authoritarian Personality*. This explains why so many leftists are totally unwilling to engage in civil discourse on the issues. They don't have to. We've already been branded. If confronted with irrefutable facts, they simply ignore them, because obviously we just don't get it. They don't need to prove anything, and we can't.

It also explains why Antifa/BLM rioters scream "Fascist, and Nazi!" at anyone who confronts them in the streets, or even just drives or walks by. If you are not with them, you are by definition one of the bad guys in need of elimination.

# Critical Race Theory

Former President Obama's favorite Harvard professor, the late Derrick Bell, devised Critical Race Theory, an offshoot of Critical Theory applied to race. According to Discover the Networks:

> *Critical race theory contends that America is permanently racist to its core, and that consequently the nation's legal structures are, by definition, racist and invalid. As Emory University professor Dorothy Brown puts it, critical race theory "seeks to highlight the ways in which the law is not neutral and objective but designed to support white supremacy and the subordination of people of color." A logical derivative of this premise, according to critical race theory, is that the members of "oppressed" racial groups are entitled—in fact obligated—to determine for themselves which laws and traditions have merit and are worth observing. Further, critical race theory holds that because racism is so deeply ingrained in the American character, classical liberal ideals such as meritocracy, equal opportunity, and colorblind justice are essentially nothing more than empty slogans that fail to properly combat—or to even acknowledge the existence of— the immense structural inequities that pervade American society and work against black people.[126]*

That is Black Lives Matter in a nutshell, and defines the extreme polarization communists have deliberately fomented in America. They couldn't achieve it by revolutionizing the proletariat, so they targeted race. Black Lives Matter leaders have referred to themselves as "trained Marxists." And Critical Race Theory is the kind of garbage they peddle.

They don't even bother to hide their true motives anymore. Dream Defenders, an organization led by Working Families Party (ACORN) activist and Occupy Wall Street anarchist Nelini Stamp, popularized the phrase "Hands Up-Don't Shoot!" which has since become BLM's widely recognized slogan. The deaths of Trayvon Martin, Michael Brown and others were mere pretexts for communist agitation. They were and are well aware that Martin and Brown were not innocent, and they also are likely aware that police killings of blacks are rarely unjustified.[127] The real enemy is "the system." This is why the BLM crowd denies the facts of those cases. As Stamp has said, "we are actually trying to change the capitalist system we have today because it's not working for any of us."[128]

More frightening, the Biden administration has adapted Critical Race Theory notions to brand our society as incurably racist. Biden's Department of Education is now seeking to install Critical Race Theory concepts into public school curriculums. It will use seed money to entice schools embrace this toxic program, indoctrinating our children against us and each other.

## White Privilege

The "racist" narrative was turbocharged with the concept of "White Privilege," the notion that whites—the dominant group in the West, and especially America, are racist, sexist, homophobic, xenophobic, *fill-in-the-blank-*phobic, imperialist oppressors who exploit everyone. Whites are the greatest evil in the world and must be exterminated.

The concept of White Privilege was created in 1967 by Noel Ignatiev, an acolyte of Bell and professor at Harvard's W.E.B. Du Bois Institute (Du Bois was a Communist black leader who helped found the NAACP). Ignatiev was a member of the Communist Party USA's most radical wing, the Maoist/Stalinist Provisional Organizing Committee to Reconstitute the Marxist-Leninist Communist Party (POC).[129]

Writing under the alias Noel Ignatin, Ignatiev co-authored an SDS pamphlet with fellow radical Ted Allen, titled *White Blindspot*. In 1992 he co-founded *Race Traitor: Journal of the New Abolitionism*. Its first issue coined the slogan, "Treason to whiteness is loyalty to humanity." Its stated objective was to "abolish the white race." More specifically, the New Abolitionist newsletter stated:

> *The way to abolish the white race is to challenge, disrupt and eventually overturn the institutions and behavior patterns that reproduce the privileges of whiteness, including the schools, job and housing markets, and the criminal justice system. The abolitionists do not limit themselves to socially acceptable means of protest, but reject in advance no means of attaining their goal.* (Emphasis added).[130]

But do not be confused; "White" does not mean white. "White" in radical construction means anyone of any race, creed, nationality, color, sex, or sexual preference who embraces capitalism, free markets, limited government and American traditional culture and values. By definition, these beliefs are irredeemably evil and anyone who aligns with them is "white" in spirit and thus equally guilty of "white crimes." Until his death in late 2020 Ignatiev taught at the Massachusetts College of Art.

The Black Lives Matter movement carries this narrative to unprecedented heights, claiming that only whites can be racists. And while justifying violence to achieve "social justice," the movement's goal is to overthrow our society to replace it with a Marxist one. Many members of the black community would be shocked to learn that the intellectual godfathers of this movement are mostly white communists, "queers" and leftist Democrats, intent on making blacks into cannon fodder for the revolution.

Following the "white privilege" narrative, in a recent speech Joe Biden called White Supremacism, "the most lethal terrorist threat to our homeland today: White supremacy is terrorism," he said.[131]

America is the most open, generous, multi-racial, multi-ethnic society in the world. Yes, we've had our problems with race in the past, but it is a situation we have worked for over a century to correct. So, the Biden administration's effort to vilify its political opponents as incurable "White Supremacists," is truly frightening. This fact alone reveals how radical this administration truly is, and how desperately we must fight against that narrative.

Biden and the Democrats have revealed their true nature. It is not yet too late to rein them in, but if the political landscape does not change soon this deliberate war against America is likely to turn hot.

# Herbert Marcuse

German Communist Herbert Marcuse was one of the better-known members of the Frankfurt School. Like almost all the prominent Marxists, Marcuse and the other Frankfurt School Communists were sons of affluence. Marcuse's father paid his rent and bought him a business, Horkheimer was the son of a millionaire and Adorno was supported by his parents. Other Frankfurt School scholars were similarly disposed. They were all "trust fund revolutionaries," totally out of touch with the real world and the "workers" with whom they pretended solidarity.[132]

Marcuse was enthusiastically received by 60s radicals (most of whom were similarly from upper class families), and was called the "Father of the New Left." He is also credited with launching the sexual revolution. As previously discussed, the intellectual forebear of that effort was Georgi Lukacs, but Marcuse popularized it in the U.S. His book *Eros and Civilization* took Freud's concept of "polymorphous perversity" and stood it on its head. Freud believed that tendency resided in all people but was and should be repressed to maintain a stable society. Marcuse instead celebrated it. He supposedly coined the phrase "Make Love not War," although he denied it. Albert Mohler writes:

> *According to Marcuse, the only way to achieve liberation is to undo that repression, to reverse that restraint, and thus to unleash in society itself that infantile stage of pure sexuality—of polymorphous perversity.*[133]

Marcuse taught at Columbia University before heading to Harvard, Brandeis, and finally the University of California, San Diego. He mentored Angela Davis, the black American Communist involved at the time with the Black Panthers, first at Brandeis, then at UC San Diego, which she attended specifically because he was there.[134]

Marcuse developed the idea of suppressing conservative speech in America in his 1965 essay "Repressive Tolerance." In order to correct the oppressive imbalance Marcuse claimed exists in Western societies, he suggested that—again recalling Lenin—those oppressed by society had a special right to conceal and suppress truth, engage in violence, law-breaking, and other civil disobedience to get their way:

> *Under the conditions prevailing in this country, tolerance does not, and cannot, fulfill the civilizing function attributed to it by the liberal protagonists of democracy, namely, protection of dissent... I believe that there is a 'natural right' of resistance for oppressed and overpowered minorities to use extralegal means if the legal ones have proved to be inadequate... If they use violence, they do not start a new chain of violence but try to break an established one.[135]*

In the sphere of public debate this meant:

> *Not "equal" but more representation of the Left would be equalization of the prevailing inequality... Given this situation, I suggested in "Repressive Tolerance" the practice of discriminating tolerance in an inverse direction, as a means of shifting the balance between Right and Left by restraining the liberty of the Right, thus counteracting the pervasive inequality of freedom (unequal opportunity of access to the means of democratic persuasion) and strengthening the oppressed against the oppressors...[136]*

Marcuse further described the types of people who needed to have their freedom curtailed:

> *[It] would include the withdrawal of toleration of speech and assembly from groups and movements which promote aggressive policies, armament, chauvinism, discrimination on the grounds of race and religion, or which oppose the extension of public services, social security, medical care, etc. Moreover, the restoration of freedom of thought may necessitate new and rigid restrictions on teachings*

*and practices in the educational institutions which, by their very methods and concepts, serve to enclose the mind within the established universe of discourse and behavior—thereby precluding a priori a rational evaluation of the alternatives.*[137]

In Marcuse's formulation, anyone who opposes, for example, programs like Social Security or Medicaid, is by definition a racist, sexist, etc. and should have his/her voice and activities silenced.

His plan came to be known as "partisan tolerance," that is tolerance only of the left's ideas and agendas. It is today practiced in newsrooms, classrooms and the public sphere generally, throughout the U.S. and the West.

## Rules for Radicals

Following Marcuse's treatise on Repressive Tolerance, American radical Saul Alinsky published one of the Left's most popular political warfare manuals, *Rules for Radicals*. This practical handbook is a how-to guide for radicals. It includes 13 rules:

1. "Power is not only what you have but what the enemy thinks you have."
2. "Never go outside the expertise of your people."
3. "Whenever possible go outside the expertise of the enemy."
4. "Make the enemy live up to its own book of rules."
5. "Ridicule is man's most potent weapon. There is no defense. It is almost impossible to counterattack ridicule. Also, it infuriates the opposition, who then react to your advantage."

6. "A good tactic is one your people enjoy."
7. "A tactic that drags on too long becomes a drag."
8. "Keep the pressure on."
9. "The threat is usually more terrifying than the thing itself."
10. "The major premise for tactics is the development of operations that will maintain a constant pressure upon the opposition."
11. "If you push a negative hard and deep enough it will break through into its counterside; this is based on the principle that every positive has its negative."
12. "The price of a successful attack is a constructive alternative."
13. "Pick the target, freeze it, personalize it, and polarize it."

The manual is very effective. Our side should use it, and some do, especially #5. "Ridicule is man's most potent weapon." Steven Crowder, Ben Shapiro, Ann Coulter and Milo Yiannopoulos have used it to great effect. But we can see what happens too. The Left's reaction is, as with much else, violent protest, threats, deplatforming and censorship. It is the most extreme example of Rule #13.

Rule #13, "Pick the target, freeze it, personalize it, and polarize it," is an application of Marcuse's partisan tolerance. We see it in use every day. The left must establish the moral high ground to get the credibility necessary to push its outrageous demands. Silencing effective voices of opposition is the first step. Then convincing the public that the Left's solution is essential to "solve" the "problem" is a necessary prerequisite to making their demands sound worthy and admirable. A successful PR campaign convincing the public that the need is genuine automatically makes opponents out to be the bad guys, and puts almost everyone on the defensive.

This narrative can then be resurrected again and again to pummel opponents into submission. Thus "racist," "sexist," "homophobe" and now "xenophobe," (for opponents of illegal alien amnesty) are really all the same negative term, "bigot," applied to any and all opponents of the Left's destruction strategies. It is simply an application of Leninism and partisan tolerance to stifle opposition. It is unethical, brutal, mean-spirited, and fundamentally dishonest (and they know it). But it is also effective, which is all they really care about. And for those whom it does not work, there is always violence.

In fact, this narrative is so effective that politicians of opposing Parties often side with the Left to avoid criticism, threats and retaliation, and reap the PR benefits of being among the "good guys." Some of these people are actually stupid enough to believe they are with the good guys, but for many it is simply a self-serving political calculation to squirm out of the Left's hostile media spotlight, while possibly benefiting politically from a voting demographic that otherwise would oppose them. Some are even offered jobs by CNN or other leftist outlets. Of course, this comes at the cost of Party unity, further legitimizes the Left's illegitimate claims, and undermines the ability to fight them off.

This is why those with any intellectual integrity hold the RINOs (Republicans in Name Only).in such utter contempt. For their part, the RINOs seek to destroy conservatives' credibility in order to further insulate themselves from the consequences of their disloyalty. Principled conservatives publicly revile them for the hypocrites they are. Of course, this destructive fracture is yet another anticipated benefit of the Left's strategy: divide and conquer.

# Orchestrated Crisis

Columbia University sociology professors Richard Cloward and Frances Fox Piven were a married team of radical socialists. Cloward died in 2001. Eighty-eight-year-old Piven still teaches at City University of New York. She was interviewed in *Jacobin* magazine in June 2020, exhorting violent protesters to, "defend their ability to exercise disruptive power."[138] Did you even know there was a "Jacobin" magazine? The Jacobins were the ones who launched the French Revolution in the late 18th Century. During the "Reign of Terror," they murdered at least 17,000 people, mostly by guillotine. Jacobinism inspired the later development of communism, socialism and anarchism, so Piven felt right at home.

Like Nechayev, Münzenberg and Lukacs, Cloward and Piven remain unknown to most Americans but they were very prominent in left-wing circles, and from the early 1960s to today they have had a profound impact on American society. Cloward and Piven were pivotal founders of many extreme Left organizations, including the National Welfare Rights Organization (NWRO) that spawned ACORN (Association of Community Organizations for Reform Now) and the Democratic Socialists of America (DSA), the U.S. arm of the Socialist International, and currently the largest communist organization in the U.S. Cloward and Piven were directly or indirectly responsible for the vast expansion of welfare, undermining the .integrity of elections and the 2008 financial crisis.

The Cloward-Piven Strategy of Manufactured Crisis, also called "break the bank" or "Crisis Strategy," was designed to deliberately create systemic crisis by overwhelming government at all levels with impossible demands for services. The hope was to foment riots when demand for services went unmet.

They outlined this strategy in a May 1966 Nation magazine article titled The Weight of the Poor: A Strategy to End Poverty.[139] Their use of "weight" had a special connotation. It was taken from Leon Trotsky, a Bolshevik and first leader of the Soviet Red Army, who equated weight with power.[140] Cloward and Piven believed that when organized as a unified force, the poor's "weight" could be "used as a battering ram against the welfare system, and by extension, against the American system itself."[141]

Cloward and Piven believed that if Americans signed up for every benefit the law entitled them to, it would overwhelm government budgets, creating a "profound financial and political crisis" that would generate demands for "major economic reform at the national level." The "reform" they envisioned was a guaranteed annual income for all Americans—socialism, in other words.

To foment this crisis, they first proposed "a massive drive to recruit the poor onto the welfare rolls." They were very specific about the kind of crisis they hoped to create:

> *By crisis, we mean a publicly visible disruption in some institutional sphere. Crisis can occur spontaneously (e.g., riots) or as the intended result of tactics of demonstration and protest which either generate institutional disruption or bring unrecognized disruption to public attention.*[142]

And,

> *Advocacy must be supplemented by organized demonstrations to create a climate of militancy that will overcome the invidious and immobilizing*

*attitudes which many potential recipients hold toward being 'on welfare.'*

In other words, Cloward and Piven deliberately sought to orchestrate a crisis that would intensify the evils and miseries of the people until they were provoked to violent action, like Nechayev advocated. Cloward and Piven-founded organizations ultimately applied their radical strategy to welfare, voting and housing. In each case, their true goal was always to find any means to institutionalize their orchestrated anarchy, and poor people were the tool.

Cloward and Piven openly acknowledged it. In creating the Crisis Strategy, Cloward and Piven asserted that welfare was not actually helping the poor, but driving them into lethargy. With the safety net, they argued, the rich had "doused the fires of rebellion."[143]

By overwhelming and bankrupting the system, Cloward and Piven hoped to drive angry welfare beneficiaries into the street, violently demanding their benefits. As Cloward told the New York Times, poor people only have power "when the rest of society is afraid of them."[144]

Their ideas helped to popularize modes of operation that have since been adopted by radicals and subversives everywhere, including, perhaps especially, our current President and Democrat politicians at all levels of government. The insanity they are inflicting on all aspects of American life today is the Crisis Strategy on steroids.

No matter where the strategy is implemented, it shares the following features:

1. The offensive organizes previously unorganized groups eligible for government benefits but not currently receiving all they can.

2. The offensive seeks to identify new beneficiaries and/or create new benefits,

3. Government funding purchases permanent new voting blocs wholesale and further solidifies current beneficiaries' support for politicians who back these policies.

4. The overarching aim is always to impose new stresses on target systems, with the ultimate goal of forcing their collapse.

The strategy accomplishes a number of complementary goals:

- Chaos makes the system difficult if not impossible to control

- Demands for services provide both actual and psychic benefits to the Left's voting demographic. To the extent that actual benefits are supplied, the Left's supporters are materially better off than they were before–temporarily.

- If all benefits cannot be supplied, the simple fact that an identifiable political organization is calling for them endears that organization to potential beneficiaries, offers a defensible—if duplicitous— justification for demanding such benefits and helps build public pressure to provide them.

Cloward and Piven were instrumental in creating the organizations that would execute this strategy, first the NWRO, under the leadership of radical activist Dr. George Wiley, and later, ACORN, headed by NWRO veteran and Students for a Democratic Society (SDS) activist, Wade Rathke. Wiley, like Ayers and so many other American radicals, was the son of a wealthy Rhode Island family. He held a PhD in chemistry from Cornell University and prior to his career as a radical was a chemistry professor at the Berkeley campus of the University of California and later at Syracuse University. Wade Rathke was from a similarly well-to-do background, although he dropped out of Williams College.

The Crisis Strategy managed to explode the welfare rolls. Between 1965 and 1974, single-parent households on welfare grew 151 percent, from 4.3 million to 10.8 million, during a period of relative economic prosperity. In New York City, where the Crisis Strategy had its greatest "success," there was one person on welfare for every two people working in the private sector.[145] This precipitated New York City's near bankruptcy in 1975. Speaking of that crisis in 1998, then-New York Mayor Rudolph Giuliani accused the pair of economic sabotage.[146]

A 1970 New York Times article reported on the disruptive activities of Wiley's NWRO:[147]

> *There have been sit-ins in legislative chambers, including a United States Senate committee hearing, mass demonstrations of several thousand welfare recipients, school boycotts, picket lines, mounted police, tear gas, arrests - and, on occasion, rock-throwing, smashed glass doors, overturned desks, scattered papers and ripped-out phones.*

Sound familiar? Author Richard Poe described the phenomenon:

> *The flood of demands was calculated to break the budget, jam the bureaucratic gears into gridlock, and bring the system crashing down. Fear, turmoil, violence and economic collapse would accompany such a breakdown—providing perfect conditions for fostering radical change. By 1969, NWRO claimed a dues-paying membership of 22,500 families, with 523 chapters across the nation.*[148]

Though they were unsuccessful in establishing a guaranteed income, ACORN has agitated for a $15 minimum wage for decades and other expansions of welfare that have largely achieved the same result through the back door. The $15 minimum wage and the guaranteed annual income are also both now being proposed by Democrats at both the state and federal level.

Cloward has been credited as the brain behind President Johnson's "War on Poverty."[149] Of course that war on poverty has entrenched both poverty and government dependence in minority communities, which in turn has made those communities toxic hotbeds of crime addiction and unwed motherhood. This was not a mistake.

Johnson was not interested in lifting minorities out of poverty, but enslaving them in government dependence to ensure their votes. He is alleged to have said, "I'll have those n*ggers voting Democratic for the next 200 years."[150] Cloward and Piven agreed. "If organizers can deliver millions of dollars in cash benefits to the ghetto masses," they wrote, "it seems reasonable to expect that the masses will deliver their loyalties to their benefactors."[151]

Johnson's program birthed the Office of Economic Opportunity. Conservative activist Howard Phillips ran OEO in 1973, and identified Cloward and Piven as OEO's "ideological architects." He said OEO financed "10,000 organizations employing several hundred thousand people" to radically transform U.S. policy outside the political process.[152] That trend has only grown since. In addition to fomenting radical change through violence and chaos, the Left has been adept at getting us to pay for it all with our own tax dollars.

## National Voter Registration Act

Cloward and Piven's next target was voting. In 1982 they created the Human Service Employees Registration and Voter Education Fund (Human SERVE) to build political momentum for a law that would turn state motor vehicle and welfare agencies into low-income voter registration offices.[153] Throughout the 1980s, Human SERVE field-tested legal and political strategies to promote this plan. The fruits of its labor were finally realized with the National Voter Registration Act of 1993 (NVRA), signed into law with Cloward and Piven standing directly behind President Clinton.

Also known as "Motor Voter," The NVRA requires motor vehicle, military recruiting, public assistance and other state and local offices to offer voter-registration services. The ACLU and other activist legal organizations sue those governments when their voter registration efforts called for by the NVRA are not vigorous enough. Consent decrees then turn those government offices into low-income voter registration drives. In states where illegal aliens can get drivers licenses, many of them wind up on the rolls as well.

 The NVRA has become a beacon for vote fraud. Its minimal verification requirements opened the door to ACORN-style massive voter registration fraud, and in the confusion provide blanket opportunities for vote fraud. The NVRA was another way to overwhelm the system, and that strategy was implemented in full force with the widespread use of often unverifiable mail-in ballots during the 2020 elections, which more than anything else, likely contributed to the result.

And while Nancy Pelosi and her congressional Democrats used the excuse of COVID to justify mail-in ballots, they had proposed universal mail-in voting two years prior. That legislation is now on the table again with Pelosi's For the People Act, H.R. 1, and its Senate companion bill, S.1. If it passes, we are unlikely to ever see a free election again.

## Subprime Mortgage Manufactured Crisis

Finally, during the 1990s ACORN worked with other activist groups to push for subprime mortgages. They were aided by the Clinton administration Department of Justice, which forced banks to offer mortgage loans whether customers were creditworthy or not. The charge was that banks were being "racist." They supposedly had engaged in a form of lending discrimination called "redlining," that is, denoting racial and ethnic zones on a map with a red line—mostly in urban areas—indicating where loans would supposedly be denied or limited regardless of the creditworthiness of residents.[154] They were accused of drawing lines around poor neighborhoods where loans would not be made. This was a practice called "redlining."

Supposedly, this inspired passage of the Community Reinvestment Act signed by President Jimmy Carter in 1977. But the entire claim was bogus. Banks, in business to make money, would not deny a creditworthy customer a loan just because of who they were or where they lived, unless they were forced to by the government. And indeed, it was government regulation that instituted redlining.

In the 1930s, the Federal Housing Administration began requiring banks to redline in order to receive FHA loan guarantees. These FHA guidelines—another titanic failure of the liberals' New Deal—were developed by President Franklin D. Roosevelt's administration and contributed mightily to urban decay for decades afterward. These rules were revoked in 1968.[155]

Activists studiously overlooked this fact in their vilification of banks. Since the CRA's passage, a number of studies have been conducted by the Richmond Federal Reserve Bank. They found no evidence of redlining to support activists' claims, and that market demand and economic risk factors played the major part in determining the quantity of mortgage loans in a given area.[156]

But as usual, the truth doesn't matter to the Left. ACORN and some of the others used the tried-and-true method of confrontational agitation, angrily occupying bank lobbies, disrupting business, terrifying customers and demonstrating on the lawns of bank executives, always with the implicit threat of violence to them and their families. Following the Republican congressional election victory in 1994, the new majority in Congress attempted to roll back the CRA law. But Democrats in Congress, in collusion with ACORN activists and the Clinton White House, prevented Republicans from enacting any reforms, and instead began aggressively expanding the program through regulatory changes.[157] Democrats resisted regulatory changes throughout the W. Bush administration as well

The Federal National Mortgage Association (Fannie Mae), a so-called government-sponsored enterprise (GSE),[158] launched a program to invest $1 trillion to guarantee mortgages for 10 million underserved families by the end of 2000. This included low and moderate-income families, minorities, "new Americans" (i.e., immigrants, including illegals), residents of central cities and rural areas, and people with special housing needs. In early 2000 another $2 trillion was promised for the next 10 years.[159] This is called socializing the risk. Banks no longer had to worry. Mortgage lending went off the charts for virtually anyone.

Then Housing Secretary, now New York Governor, Andrew Cuomo acknowledged that this would increase mortgage lending risk, but said it was worth the effort.[160] Using the GSEs, the Clinton administration and congressional Democrats got the government to underwrite the risk.[161] The predictable bubble and burst soon followed. This was a deliberate Crisis strategy. It took until 2008 for the bubble to burst, which likely helped win the election for Barack Obama.

## Barack Obama and Joe Biden

Prior to Biden, the Obama administration was far-and-away the most radical ever. Obama himself was mentored for eight years as a youth by Communist Party USA member and probable Soviet agent Frank Marshal Davis.[162] Obama's administration was largely comprised of Communists related in one way or another to Communists Davis knew during his time in Chicago.[163]

As President, Obama applied the Crisis Strategy to practically everything he did. His trillion dollar "stimulus" promised "shovel ready" infrastructure jobs, but only about $5 billion (a mere 0.5 percent) was actually ever spent on infrastructure jobs, and we're not even sure about that. Most of the money went instead to bail out Democrat states that had overspent. $80 billion in the "Green Energy" program largely went to friends, political allies and donors in the energy business. Obama's stimulus mostly stimulated Democrats.

Obama also almost single-handedly instigated the war on police that skyrocketed during his administration. While he condemned events like the ambush killings of five police officers in Dallas during a Black Lives Matter protest in 2016, those kinds of things were happening because his rhetoric blamed police for disparate treatment of blacks in the criminal justice system. He was aided and abetted by the Eric Holder Department of Justice, which refused to prosecute obvious crimes committed by blacks.

The man who murdered those five policemen and injured many more stated that "he was upset by police shootings, referenced Black Lives Matter, and stated that he wanted to kill White people, especially White police officers."[164] In 2016, killings of police increased 61 percent.[165]

William Johnson, executive director of the National Association of Police Organizations, said in a Fox News interview:

> *I think [the Obama administration] continued appeasements at the federal level with the Department of Justice, their appeasement of violent criminals, their refusal to condemn movements like Black Lives Matter, actively calling for the death of police officers, that type of thing, all the while blaming police for the problems in this country has led directly to the climate that has made Dallas possible...*
>
> *I think one of the big differences then was you had governors and mayors and the president — whether it was President Johnson or President Nixon, Republican or Democrat — condemning violence against the police and urging support for the police. Today that's markedly absent. I think that's a huge difference, and that's directly led to the climate that allows these attacks to happen.*
>
> *It's a war on cops... And the Obama administration is the Neville Chamberlain of this war.*[166]

What are the facts? Police, whether white or black, do not single out blacks because they are racist. In fact, police are less likely to shoot a black person than a white person precisely because of the negative blowback. According to Rep. Mo Brooks (R-AL), "A 2016 Harvard University study by African American Professor Roland

Fryer, Jr., found that police fire upon African Americans 24 percent less often than police fire upon Caucasian Americans."[167]

Yet Obama claimed that ``Black folks are more vulnerable to these kinds of incidents."[168] It is true that blacks are targeted by police more frequently than any other demographic. Is that evidence of "systemic racism?" Hardly. *It is because blacks commit violent crime wildly out of proportion to their relative proportion in the population.* Key facts; blacks represent 13 percent of the U.S. population, yet:

1. On average, 40 percent of all police officers feloniously killed are killed by blacks. This has been true for decades.[169]
2. In 2019 blacks killed 566 whites while whites killed 246 blacks.[170] These kinds of numbers are consistent year over year. If blacks represented 61 percent of the population as whites now do, what do you think that statistic would look like?
3. From 2010 to 2019, of known offenders, more blacks were arrested for murder and non-negligent homicide, (about 51 percent of the total) than any other group.[171] This represents a total of 60,389 murders.[172]
4. 93 percent of all murders of blacks are committed by other blacks, every year.[173]
5. Police kill twice as many whites each year as they do blacks, despite disproportionate police deaths at the hands of blacks and much higher crime rates among blacks.

Now, knowing all this, who would you expect to get more attention from the police? If you were a police officer, who would you be more worried about? Former President Obama, Eric Holder and other race hustlers decry the fact that 40 percent of our prison population is black, but given the proportion of crimes committed by blacks, it should actually be higher.

With the "defund the police" movement gaining traction, the number of black-on-black murders and the overall murder rate generally, shot way up in 2020. These statistics will only get worse as Black Lives Matter continues to excuse black violence and blame everyone else, while that fraudulent narrative is hyped by its supporters in education, politics and the media.

What you need to understand is that this effort to abolish local police is not really intended to get rid of all police. *It is an effort to federalize the police so they can be turned to the revolutionary purpose.* The FBI is looking more and more like the KGB every day. No one is protesting them.

The Biden administration has turbocharged the Crisis strategy now in evidence everywhere, with illegal aliens flooding the border in record numbers and government spending off the charts. Biden has strangled production of carbon fuels and the jobs that go with it by suspending construction of the Keystone pipeline, while at the same time lifting Trump-imposed sanctions on construction of the Russian Nord Stream 2 gas pipeline to Germany. This mere weeks after the Russians launched a cyberattack on the U.S. Colonial pipeline that shut down gasoline supplies to the entire east coast. U.S. Embassies now fly the Black Lives Matter flag. To the uninitiated it looks like the whole world has gone insane, but they are crazy like a fox.

As of this writing, Biden and the Democrats have proposed over $6 trillion in spending, of which $1.9 trillion has already been enacted with the American Rescue Plan.

$350 billion of this will actually go to once again "rescue" state budgets in the red due to irresponsible spendthrift governors and legislators in mostly Democrat-controlled states.

Consider that while most people are anxious to receive their $1,400 COVID relief payment, it will cost the average taxpayer about $4,000 in taxes to get it. And they are the lucky ones. The top 10 percent of income earners pay about 70 percent of all income taxes. They will be forking out much more to pay for all this and get nothing for it. But don't worry; Biden and Co. are handling it by simply printing money. This has already resulted in dramatic price increases, and we are likely to see much more as inflation spikes.

In 2020 the election was overwhelmed with fraudulent mail-in votes and a Democrat Party intent on instituting massive changes to secure themselves a permanent majority. Their management of COVID was calculated to make President Trump look bad, which included a shocking, unprecedented conspiracy by Democrats, media, Dr. Fauci, other health officials and the pharmaceutical industry to prevent the use of simple, inexpensive remedies like hydroxychloroquine and Ivermectin.[174]

Many people may have died because of it, but that didn't matter to the Left. Antifa/BLM caused countless billions in damage and death with their nonstop street violence. And mask mandates certainly didn't apply to them. Democrats said and did nothing. So, should we be surprised at what we see now?

President Biden is a weak, politically compromised person at best, and almost certainly cognitively impaired. But Joe has always been a leftist; never a "moderate" as many believe. Biden owes his political fortunes to the Council for a Livable World, a far-left organization founded by Leo Szilard.

Szilard was a scientist on the Manhattan Project that developed the atomic bomb. He was fingered, along with Robert Oppenheimer and Enrico Fermi, as providing *"The most vital information for developing the first Soviet atomic bomb,"* according to Pavel Sudaplatov, a member of an elite "Special Tasks" unit of Soviet intelligence.[175]

As documented in *White House Reds*, by noted author and film-maker Trevor Loudon, Biden's entire career has been spent on the far-left political spectrum. He opposed Reagan's missile defense and always took the Soviet side on issues related to nuclear deterrence. He also opposed our efforts to stop the spread of communism in Central America.[176] Biden himself admitted as much in a speech to South American leftist leaders at the "Progressive Governance Summit" held in Chile in 2009:

> *President Obama and I sought these offices because we had a fundamental disagreement with the policies of the last administration… And it's a little bit like that old metaphor—it takes a while to turn around a super-tanker. We are moving as rapidly as we can to change the direction of our country and our policies, but we're going to have to ask… for a little bit of patience as we move forward.[177]*

Today they are wasting no time. Every single agenda proposed by the Biden administration is the most radical ever attempted. He would not oppose any of it, but given his rapidly advancing dementia and clearly ill health, it is apparent that someone else is pulling the puppet strings. That person is Barack Obama and his crew of Communists and Socialists who wreaked havoc in our nation—with Biden's help—for Obama's entire eight years. Obama recently admitted as much, saying, "I think that what we're seeing now is Joe and the administration are essentially finishing the job."[178]

## Black Lives Matter and Antifa

Black Lives Matter (BLM) launched in 2013 with a Twitter hashtag, #BlackLivesMatter, after neighborhood watchman George Zimmerman was acquitted in the Trayvon Martin killing. Radical Left activists Alicia Garza, Patrisse Cullors and Opal Tometi claim credit for the slogan and hashtag. Following the Michael Brown shooting in August 2014, Dream Defenders, an organization led by Working Families Party (ACORN) activist and Occupy Wall Street anarchist Nelini Stamp, popularized the phrase "Hands Up-Don't Shoot!" which has since become BLM's widely recognized slogan.[179] Stamp revealed BLM's true goals when she said, "we are actually trying to change the capitalist system we have today because it's not working for any of us."[180]

Both BLM and Antifa are Communist/Anarchist groups whose stated goal is to overthrow capitalism. Patrisse Cullors made a video that has since gone viral, where she admits BLM's Marxist roots, she says:

> *We do have an ideological frame. Myself and Alicia, in particular, are trained organizers; we are trained Marxists. We are superversed on, sort of, ideological theories. And I think what we really try to do is build a movement that could be utilized by many, many Black folks.[181]*

Some have objected to that characterization of the movement, claiming it represents a broad swath of people, most of whom are not communists. The leftwing "fact" checker Politifact noted that BLM has a nationwide following simply based on the sentiment.[182]

This is all no doubt true, but the effect is the same, because it is the leaders who call the shots. As Whittaker Chambers warned us, the great danger of communism is that most of its followers are not communists. They are advocates and do-gooders of every stripe who don't know or don't care about the organization's pedigree. They embrace the narrative, thinking that the party affiliation of its leaders is irrelevant.

With communist organizations, the communist goals are the *only thing that matters*. It is just dressed up in the flowery language of "compassion," "social justice," or some other nebulous term that sounds good. Whether Lenin said it or not, the people who get caught up in this really are idiots. Recall Willi Münzenberg's words:

> *"We must avoid being a purely communist organization...We must bring in other names, other groups, to make persecution more difficult." Middle-class opinion makers, liberal sympathizers, however much echt [genuine] Bolsheviks despised them, must be used.*

And of course, Münzenberg was just paraphrasing Nechayev, who said: "*The revolutionary must pretend to collaborate with them...*"

That is the significance of Cullors' claim to be a "trained Marxist." The ideas, strategies and goals outlined in this book are the kind of training "trained Marxists" get. Furthermore, the riots BLM and Antifa have been involved with, beginning with George Floyd, were launched on false pretenses. The radicals were just looking for an excuse. In every case, police were following standards for the scenarios they found themselves in. Derek Chauvin may have overdone it, but the knee on the neck was recommended procedure for a noncompliant arrestee. George Floyd likely died of Fentanyl poisoning. And riots spawned by BLM and Antifa resulted in many more deaths of blacks than those they were allegedly protesting.

BLM is actually a project of Liberation Road, an offshoot of the Freedom Road Socialist Organization

(FRSO). The Minneapolis-based FRSO actually bragged about instigating the George Floyd riots. Organizer Jess Sundlin was thrilled when rioters burned down police third district headquarters, "I can't tell you the joy it brought all of us to see the Third Precinct destroyed," she said.[183]

Many reporters sought to distinguish rioters and looters as small, marginalized groups within the "mostly peaceful" protest movement, arguing that there was no relation between these groups. Sundlin makes clear that was absolutely false:

> There has been a lot of confusion sown ... about whether those night demonstrations are in fact legitimate. And I want to be absolutely clear as an organizer—what I did most of the last three weeks was organize rallies ... and marches—those night demonstrations, the emptying of the Police Department, the emptying of Target and other major stores ... is absolutely tied to, connected to, and part of the movement.[184]

If as Nelini Stamp has said, they want to overthrow capitalism, wouldn't they be more likely to sympathize with the Communist Chinese than America? And indeed, they do. Both Liberation Road and FRSO are Maoist, Communist organizations that openly support the Chinese Communist Party. This is important because Liberation Road is allied with the San Francisco-based Chinese Progressive Association (CPA), which has close ties to Red China's consulate in San Francisco. BLM founder Alicia Garza runs Black Future Labs Project, an organization funded by CPA.[185] And Communist China has actually been directing some of the BLM/Antifa riots behind the scenes.[186]

For example, the Chinese consulate in Houston was closed last year when it was discovered it housed a Chinese Red Army intelligence unit that was identifying potential BLM/Antifa rioters, contacting them through social media and sending them videos about how to riot.

Chinese Communists have also deeply penetrated our many institutions.[187] Next to Mexico and Central America, Immigrants from China are the largest group given legal permanent residence in the U.S. Every year, about 76,000 Chinese legally immigrate to the U.S. They are all beholden to the old country, no matter how much they might prefer being here. They wouldn't be allowed to leave China otherwise. Even those who thoroughly embrace American society will have relatives in China essentially held hostage to make sure they know where their loyalties lie. Chinese government officials at consulates in the U.S. can at any time contact these people and expect whatever cooperation they require.

In one 2018 case, Chinese intelligence officers working out of China's San Francisco Consulate bussed in between 6,000 and 8,000 Chinese students in California on J-Visas (for scholars, professors and exchange visitors) to disrupt an anti-Chinese government rally in San Francisco held by members of the Chinese Falun Gong religious group, Tibetan, and Uighur dissidents and others.[188]

We essentially have a Communist Chinese fifth column operating in the U.S. today, with hundreds of thousands of people willing to do China's bidding. According to national defense expert Bill Gertz, there are approximately 25,000 Chinese spies in the U.S. 5,000 of these came in after 2012 as students, businessmen, or immigrants. Another 18,000 Americans of Chinese and other ethnic origin have been recruited by Chinese intelligence. So, we're looking at the possibility of over 40,000 Chinese espionage agents and spies in the U.S.[189]

These people are today working in government, universities, research facilities and our political system. More have been bought off politically and are beholden to the Chinese Communists, including, almost certainly, the current sitting President.

BLM groups have also joined with the Communist Party USA, DSA, SEIU, Color of Change and many others extremists. Anarchist and top Occupy Wall Street (OWS) organizer Lisa Fithian, who orchestrated the 1999 Seattle World Trade Organization riots, trained Ferguson protesters. Echoing Cloward and Piven, Fithian says "Create crisis, because crisis is that edge where change is possible." No one called them "Antifa" then, but those white anarchists and communists led by Fithian helped burn Ferguson to the ground.

## Antifa

 Pictured here is current Minnesota Attorney General and former DNC Deputy Chairman Keith Ellison. This photo surfaced as Antifa and BLM were burning Minneapolis to the ground. Later Ellison took over the prosecution of Derek Chauvin and the other officers charged in George Floyd's death. Do you think they are getting fair trials? His son Jeremiah serves on the Minneapolis City Council and proposed and passed a referendum to abolish the Minneapolis police shortly after George Floyd's death. Minneapolis crime has soared in 2020, in some wards by as much as 74 percent.[190]

Antifa is virtually indistinguishable from BLM in its outlook and goals, except that its members are largely white. It gets its name from "Antifaschistische Aktion," a 1930s communist group that clashed in the streets with Nazi Brown Shirts. Today it is a confederation of communists, anarchists and other radicals, in many cases led and paid for by professional agitators. The same types were out in force during the Occupy Wall Street protests, and earlier, during the Seattle World Trade Organization meeting in 1999 where they torched automobiles and clashed with police. They've been around for a while, whatever they call themselves now, as described in the following article from the Claremont Institute's *American Mind*:

> *According to Antifa lore, an effort by young punks to expel neo-Nazis and white supremacists from the music scene led to the formation of Anti-Racist Action (ARA), beginning in the Midwest and then spreading outward. As chapters formed in various cities, regional councils and networks were formed, such as the Midwest Anti-Fascist Network (MAFN) in 1995.*
>
> *But present at the birth of ARA were members of America's long-time revolutionary clique, with roots going all the way back to the domestic terror group Weather Underground. Consulting the young anti-racist punks in the formation of ARA were members of the John Brown Anti-Klan Committee (JBAKC). Several separate ARAs would go on to form one of the largest Antifa networks in the country, Torch Antifa, whose website was registered by a former JBAKC member.*
>
> *JBAKC was formed as a front for the May 19th Communist Organization (MCO), itself founded out of the remnants of the Weather Underground, Black Liberation Army, the FALN and other terrorist groups of the '60s and '70s. (May 19 was chosen since it was the birthday of both Malcolm X and Ho Chi Minh.)*
>
> *Following a split in the Weather Underground leadership over whether to emphasize class or racial struggle, the MCO emphasized working for "black liberation." Members of the MCO were responsible*

*for several bombings and robberies in the 1980s, including the infamous 1981 Brinks Armored Car Robbery.[191]*

The MCO it should be noted, included Susan Rosenberg, a true insurrectionist who participated in numerous bombings in 1983 and 1984, including at the National War College, an FBI office, the U.S. Capitol and other targets.[192] She avoided prosecution for her role in those bombings through a plea agreement, but in 1985 was sentenced to 58 years for explosives possession. Her sentence was commuted by Bill Clinton in 2001 just before he left office. Rosenberg now sits on the board of Thousand Currents, the tax-exempt organization that until very recently funded Black Lives Matter.[193] So here we are today. It comes full circle. These groups are all communist-oriented and dedicated to the violent overthrow of America as they have been proving for decades.

Antifa uses cellular structures similar to trained communist guerrilla organizations, pointing to the fact that many members are "trained Marxists." Rigorous steps are taken to thoroughly vet new members.

CrimethInc.com is an Anarchist website that describes how to create an Antifa group in a post titled, *How to Organize an Affinity Group.* This is more for the useful idiots than the true revolutionaries. They have their own guidance.

*Turbulent times are upon us. Already, blockades, demonstrations, riots, and clashes are occuring [sic] regularly. It's past time to be organizing for the upheavals that are on the way. But getting organized doesn't mean joining a pre-existing institution and taking orders. It shouldn't mean forfeiting your agency and intelligence to become a cog in a machine. From an anarchist perspective, organizational structure should maximize both freedom and voluntary coordination at every level of scale, from the smallest group up to society as a whole. You and your friends already constitute an affinity group, the essential building block of this model. An affinity group is a circle of friends who understand themselves as an autonomous political force. The idea is that people who already know and trust each other should work together to respond immediately, intelligently, and flexibly to emerging situations. This leaderless format has proven effective for guerrilla activities of all kinds, as well as what the RAND Corporation calls "swarming" tactics in which many unpredictable autonomous groups overwhelm a centralized adversary. You should go to every demonstration in an affinity group, with a shared sense of your goals and capabilities. If you are in an affinity group that has experience taking action together, you will be much better prepared to deal with emergencies and make the most of unexpected opportunities...*[194]

Note that this article predicts growing unrest. Since Antifa and BLM have been the ones instigating that unrest, we should heed the warning. But this has actually been building for decades. Occupy Wall Street may have been a warm-up for what has been happening since last year. Expect to see more and worse, unless the political landscape changes dramatically soon in America's favor.

## Border Crisis and the Role of the UN

Few words are needed to describe the crisis at the border, other than to say it is unprecedented. In April 2021 alone, 178,622 illegal aliens were apprehended by Border Patrol, a

20 year high. So far this year, 531,533 illegals have been apprehended, and those were the ones caught. This almost equals total apprehensions for all of the last calendar year, 547,819, and those numbers were also very high.[195] But under President Trump, the Remain in Mexico program assured that most of those aliens would not stay here. Under Biden, these people are being housed, fed and bussed or flown to destinations of their choosing within the U.S. Few, if any, will ever appear in court for asylum hearings as required. The waiting time as of this writing is 934 days.[196]

We've all heard about cartel-sponsored human traffickers raping illegal females and forcing them into prostitution, men being forced into indentured servitude, MS-13 gangs recruiting boys and many other horror stories. Cartel members mock the Border Patrol from across the border, while BP officers are forced to care for aliens that come across, leaving wide gaps in the border open to drug smuggling and human trafficking.

The administration recently made a token gesture by agreeing to allow 13.5 miles of the border fence to be completed. But even that is a fraud. The section to be completed is a levee system to prevent flooding along the Rio Grande River. Gaps left in the actual wall will remain open.[197] Another 103 miles of border wall have been funded but that construction has not resumed.

Biden's actions are an outrage and have generated heated response from both Republican and Democrat politicians representing border communities. This state of affairs is unlikely to change unless enormous pressure is brought to bear on the Biden administration. After all this is a key component of the Crisis Strategy. Joe Biden has no intention of letting up.

But the open borders agenda has actually been in place in one form or another since the 1960s. The late Senator Ted Kennedy sponsored both the 1965 Immigration and Nationalities Act and the 1980 Refugee Act. Both were designed to turbocharge immigration from third world countries, many of whose immigrants would be attracted to America's generous welfare system, and of course vote for politicians promising more, as the Democrats always do. Kennedy was assisted in promoting the INA by leaders of the California Communist Party, whom he had befriended when they supported the presidential candidacy of JFK. In fact, some of the INA's provisions reflected the communists' demands.[198]

Democrat politicians have also encouraged illegal immigration for decades. In the 1980s for example, one-fifth of El Salvador's population came to the U.S., almost all illegally. Over the decades this mass immigration has gradually shifted voting demographics, putting more and more states in the D column. This has happened in California, Colorado, New Mexico and Virginia. It is happening in Georgia, Arizona and even Texas. If amnesty granted illegals the right to vote, Texas would turn blue overnight and we would never see a Republican elected President again.

The migrant caravans now storming our borders aren't spontaneous. They're highly organized and are being assisted by multiple U.S. based tax-exempt organizations, some of which get government funding. For example, the Illinois Coalition for Immigrant and Refugee Rights (ICIRR) gets 80 percent of its funding from the state of Illinois. ICIRR distributed $11,000 to $246,000 in government grant money to each of 59 separate organizations for "Immigrant and Refugee Rights" in 2017 alone.[199]

Another extreme Left organization helping out is the National Lawyers Guild, labeled a Communist front by Congress decades ago. It's a subsidiary of the International Association of Democratic Lawyers, founded as a Soviet propaganda front. NLG brings volunteer attorneys to help caravan migrants with asylum applications.[200]

In 2018, five UN agencies were stationed in Central America to assist the massive migrant caravans coming north. The UN provided food, shelter, busses to the border and counseling on answers illegals should give to border officials once they arrived at our border.[201] One of those UN agencies is the International Office of Migration (IOM). On its own website IOM describes its services to migrants:[202]

> **1. Information delivery:** Information is provided on the services for which migrants have access to along the route: assistance services and shelters in the region, among others. For example, the MigApp application provides georeferencing and other useful information for access to migration regularization mechanisms, humanitarian visas or other permits that may be provided by the transit and destination countries.
> **2. Strengthening the capabilities of authorities assisting caravan migrants**: IOM has provided a series of hygiene and food kits at different points where caravans pass.
> **3. Aid in voluntary assisted return for those migrants who decide to return to their communities of origin**: Migrants often voluntarily decide to return after they realize the difficulties of the route, run out of available money, fall ill, or spend a long time waiting for visas and asylum, among other reasons. IOM facilitates a safe and dignified return, in some cases with support post-arrival. The voluntary character is crucial for this axis.
> **4. Collection of data on the population:** This axis intersects with all the work carried out by the IOM, which has as its main objective the characterization of the migrant profiles, in order to channel their assistance and operation more effectively.

For the uninitiated, the UN is a communist organization. It has been since the day its charter was written by U.S. State Department bureaucrat and secret Soviet agent Alger Hiss in 1945.[203] Every single UN Secretary-General since its founding has been either a Communist or a Socialist. It is currently headed by Antonio Guterres, formerly the UN High Commissioner for Refugees (UNHCR). Guterres is a lifelong Socialist, former head of the Socialist International and former Socialist Prime Minister of Portugal.[204]

For just one small example, Taryn Fivek is a public information officer at the aforementioned IOM. Fivek is also an organizer for the Workers World (Communist) Party Her blog is titled *All Power to the Soviets*. The most recent post is *Hope in the Belly of the Beast: NYC Commemoration of Bolshevik Revolution.* "What gives us hope?" Fivek asks. "We know that we will win. That's revolutionary optimism…"[205]

The U.S. contributes more to the UN budget than any other country, despite the fact that almost all UN activities are directed against us. We contribute almost 40 percent of the UNHCR budget.[206] Lenin said "The capitalists will sell us the rope with which to hang them." The truth is that we are buying the rope they will hang us with, and giving it to them on a silver platter.

In a subsequent monograph this author will explain how the migrant caravans, that actually began with an explosion of child migration in 2012 were instigated deliberately by the Obama administration, with Joe Biden as point man to carry out this subversive strategy. In Guatemala, the Obama administration arm-twisted the government, including the threat of withdrawing promised financial aid, to force the appointment of communist guerrilla sympathizers into the highest levels of the legal system. These people shielded guerrillas still operating in the countryside following the 36-year civil war, who increased crime and poverty deliberately. At the same time Obama announced the DACA (Deferred Action for Childhood Arrivals) and DAPA (Deferred Action for Parents of Americans) programs, essentially declaring the borders open to people seeking escape from these worsening conditions.

## COVID 19 and the Great Reset

In the early 2000s Chinese Communist General Chi Haotian gave a secret speech to Chinese Communist Party leaders where he outlined the strategy and justification for using biological warfare against the U.S. with a weaponized superbug. In the speech, Chi describes how China's population growth cannot be contained within the borders of China. This, and nationalistic themes eerily reminiscent of Hitler, is used to justify China's intended takeover of America, where Americans will be given a choice: leave or die. He said:

> *Conventional weapons such as fighters, canons, missiles and battleships won't do; neither will highly destructive weapons such as nuclear weapons. We are not as foolish as to want to perish together with America by using nuclear weapons... Only by using non-destructive weapons that can kill many people will we be able to reserve America for ourselves. There has been rapid development of modern biological technology, and new bio-weapons have been invented one after another. Of course, we have not been idle, in the past years we have seized the opportunity to master weapons of this kind. We are capable of achieving our purpose of "cleaning up" America all of a sudden... Biological weapons are unprecedented in their ruthlessness, but if the Americans do not die then the Chinese have to die...*

*It is indeed brutal to kill one or two hundred million Americans. But that is the only path that will secure a Chinese century in which the CCP leads the world...*[207]

This was before 2003. They have doubtless made much progress since then. The current SARS virus, COVID-19, was almost certainly a bioweapon, manufactured in Wuhan's Biosafety Level 4 laboratory.[208] Recall that the original SARS epidemic also came from China. This is not a coincidence. In a January 2020 Netflix documentary titled "Pandemic," Dr Dennis Carroll, director of the Emerging Threats Unit at the US Agency for International Development, warned: "While we can't predict where the next influenza pandemic is going to come from, there are certain places that need particular attention—and China is one of those. It's the place where we have seen the emergence of virtually all of the deadly influenza viruses over the last half-century."[209]

Some believe the COVID-19 outbreak was deliberate. While they shut down travel within China, the Communists allowed air travel to continue, thereby deliberately contaminating the world with the virus, killing almost 3.4 million people to date and shattering the world economy.

A lot could be said for this theory. It may have been a distraction to take the world's eyes off Hong Kong, where the Communists have been suppressing the pro-freedom protesters and completing their takeover. Also, President Trump was the first president to actually stand up to the Communist Chinese. What better way to derail his efforts and poison his reelection prospects than by inflicting this national emergency?

It may have been so, but was more likely an erroneously leaked germ that was not yet ready for prime time. First, we learned of the leak from a brave Chinese doctor who later died of COVID-19.[210] Then the Chinese

Communists moved into CYA overdrive, shutting everything down and pointing fingers at the U.S.—classic communist face-saving actions. A deliberate release would have been better hidden and the virus would have been more virulent, as this secret speech makes clear would be their intention.

That said, the communists took every opportunity to capitalize on this crisis. The Chinese blamed the U.S., refused to share the vaccine they quickly developed and the American Left and Democrat Party did everything they could to shift the blame on President Trump—even up to vilifying and preventing the use of promising treatments like hydroxychloroquine, which could have saved many lives in the U.S. as it did overseas.[211]

President Trump made unprecedented efforts to address the problem. He mobilized the private sector to provide ventilators, masks and other critical supplies almost overnight, facilitated development of effective virus inoculations in record time and set up a schedule for rapid distribution. Biden just waltzed in and took the credit, giving President Trump none. Ask yourself if, during an election year, with the economy spinning like a top, Democrats would have risked shutting down the economy just because of some little old virus? They are willing to sabotage anything in service to their agenda, or take credit for good things they had nothing to do with. This *is* today's Democrat Party.

The shutdowns actually served the Left's purpose. The Left never does a cost/benefit analysis of their plans because they are uninterested in the costs. The shutdowns were arguably as destructive to life and liberty as COVID was—even more destructive. Small business is the true engine of economic growth. So, while large stores like Walmart, other big box stores and large chain grocery stores remained open, small businesses serving the community were shuttered. Many went out of business and those businesses were absorbed for a pittance by the chains. Suicides, drug addiction, crime and disease spiked.

Meanwhile, across the globe we keep hearing about the "Great Reset." Globalist organizations, in coordination with the UN see the pandemic as a grand opportunity to restructure the world economy along Marxist lines. "Never let a good crisis go to waste," as Obama Chief-of-Staff Rahm Emmanuel, echoing Cloward and Piven, once said.

Australian MP Craig Kelly called it "one of the greatest threats" facing our freedoms and our democracy. He says the tactics they are using are identical to the global warming scare:

> *We have a group of global elites that have taken over all these UN bureaucracies that at their core are Marxist and socialist...We've got to call this out for what it is, and we've got to push back very very darn hard on it. It's all about sensationalism, creating these grave threats sometime in the future, creating panic in society, hoping the people will actually surrender their freedoms, and hoping that weak politicians will surrender their nation's sovereignty to these UN power-hungry bureaucrats.*[212]

He is right. But it goes deeper than that. As mentioned earlier, the UN is essentially a communist organization. Its purpose from the beginning was to advance the international communist movement under the banner of "one world government." The Soviets always saw the UN as an instrument of their foreign policy. It was deliberately created that way by Alger Hiss and his small group of fellow communists.[213] All of those organizations clamoring for the "great reset" are similarly disposed. Is this because they really believe a world government would improve economic conditions and "save the oppressed of the earth?"

No. Of course not. As we now know, the Left everywhere is greedy for power. And those at the top see themselves glorified in unlimited power and wealth. They want to make a heaven here for themselves that will be a hell for everyone else, and as Marx said,

> *I will wander godlike and victorious*
> *Through the ruins of the world*
> *And, giving my words an active force,*
> *I will feel equal to the Creator.*

That is the true essence of communism. They think they can replace God. But instead, they just act out what they are at the core: entrepreneurial parasites; greedy, manipulative, megalomaniacal psychopaths. This has been demonstrated by the leaders in every single communist country in the world.

However, those nations have only survived because Western economic assistance has kept them afloat. Two institutions that have repeatedly bailed out failed communist states are the World Bank and International Monetary Fund. These organizations were created by another Soviet agent, Harry Dexter White, a Treasury Department official under FDR who was later appointed by President Truman to create these entities. But the U.S. has continually loaned money to Russia, given money to terrorist states like Iran and the Palestinian territories, and U.S. corporations built most of China's manufacturing infrastructure, profits from which they have now turned into weapons against us.

But America remains both the breadbasket to the world and the consumer market to the world. During the Great Depression of the 1930s, U.S. GNP fell 25 percent. World industrial production fell 30 percent, ushering in World War II. If the Left is successful in destroying our nation, the main generator of world wealth will collapse, and with it the entire world economic edifice will collapse. The Great Depression will look like a walk in the park by comparison. Most, if not all of those horrible people will be swept up in the revolutionary storm. It will be an end times calamity. Given that fact, one struggles to comprehend their determination. It cannot be comprehended rationally; their agenda is literally insane.

# All Roads Still Lead to Moscow

Our eyes are all on China, its rapidly growing military and overwhelming influence within our country. We are worried about Iran and the ongoing conflicts in the Middle East. For a long time, we worried about al Qaeda. Where did they go? But just recently, Russian hackers took down the Colonial gasoline pipeline, causing dramatically spiked fuel prices amidst all the other energy related economic chaos created by the Biden administration.

Biden seems so intent on ending carbon energy one might almost be tempted to think they are working together. And it appears they are, but not to end use of carbon fuels, given Biden's decision to lift the sanctions that blocked completion of the Russia's gas pipeline. Apparently, we must be punished for using fossil fuels—but not the Russians.

What on earth, you ask? If you believed the Democrats in 2016, the Russians "hacked the election" to benefit Trump, and the two of them working together were a threat to national security!

But wait. They haven't forgotten. They are still going after Trump and still claiming he worked with the Russians, despite two impeachments and four years of investigations that proved otherwise. It's like a broken record.

As the Soviets said in 1943, tell the same lie over and over and eventually it will become truth in the public eye. It was Democrats who claimed the embarrassing Hillary/Podesta emails were hacked by the Russians. This has not been proved. A story circulated initially that they were leaked by DNC staffer Seth Rich to Wikileaks, but in public interviews, Julian Assange has not confirmed that.[214] Rich was murdered gangland style in DC under suspicious circumstances. The investigation has gone nowhere—

claiming it was a robbery gone bad, even though nothing was taken.

The Democrats have been obsessed with Russia. All we've heard from them for the last four years is "Russia! Russia! Russia!" But it was the Democrats who used Russian disinformation to concoct the ridiculous "Steele Dossier." It was Hillary who sold 20 percent of our uranium producing capability to the Russians—with no oversight. It was Obama who told Russian President Medvedev he would have more freedom to disarm our nuclear capability, "after my election."[215] The Democrats have always been a much better bet for the Russians.

So where did Russia go? It appears we are all friends now.

Any serious national security expert will tell you that China is the existential threat. China has been much more aggressive on the world stage, is building its military rapidly in plain sight and working assiduously behind the scenes to infiltrate and corrupt our institutions. So, is China our greatest threat? It certainly appears to be. Russia is rarely mentioned. After all, we won the Cold War, didn't we?

Did we? In terms of military strength China rates well behind the U.S. and Russia, with America #1 and Russia not far behind. So why is Russia dismissed as of no concern? While our nuclear deterrent has been decaying for decades, they modernized their missile fleet. The chart below shows Russia ahead of us in sheer numbers, and many of those missiles have better capability than ours.

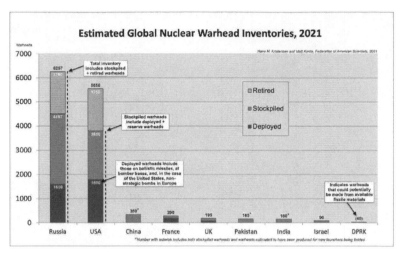

Source: Federation of American Scientists

To the extent that we know their capabilities, the Russian military compares very favorably with ours. Their troop strength is much larger, 3.5 million compared to our 2.2 active duty and reservists. But we have been fighting wars for 20 years. Our small volunteer force is exhausted. They are tanned, rested and ready. Theoretically we can call up 120 million "fit for service" young people, but how do you think a draft would go over with this "Woke" generation? Antifa? BLM? Those riots would go postal. Russia supposedly only has 46 million fit for service, but not one of them is woke, and protesting service will get you the Gulag, comrade.

Russia has overwhelming firepower in many conventional weapons compared to the U.S.: 13,000 tanks compared to our 6,100; 11,000 artillery pieces to our 2,800; 603 ships to our 490. We have a few more submarines, 68 to their 64, but their anti-submarine force is much larger than ours.[216] Our carrier fleet, 11 ships, is the largest in the world.

Russia has only one carrier, but both Russia and China have developed weapons to destroy our carriers in a shooting war. They have chosen fewer carriers because of the cost and because they know carriers are vulnerable. We have many more fighter aircraft, 1,956 to their 789, but our air forces— and all elements of our military for that matter—are highly reliant on GPS and other vulnerable high-tech electronics. The Russians and Chinese alike intend to destroy them at the start of any significant shooting war.

For example, micro circuitry purchased from China was found to contain backdoor Trojans with which the Chinese could shut down their functioning with the flip of a switch.[217] This story has been disputed by some, but those disputes sound suspiciously self-serving. Hopefully that problem has been corrected. Russia and China have also pioneered in the development of satellite countermeasures that could take down our GPS and communications system at the start of any shooting war. We are working on countermeasures,[218] and President Trump recognized this threat by launching a new U.S. Space Force—yet another unrecognized accomplishment of this president. Will Biden and the Democrats support it? They fought missile defense for decades.

But even more importantly, we do not honestly know how advanced all their capabilities are. The fact is that we have really dropped the ball. The Russians are practicing the games they always have, which are based on the strategies of 2,000-year-old military philosopher Sun Tzu. Sun says, "All warfare is deception...When strong appear weak...When near appear far...", and similar ideas.

That strategy has worked. We have ignored them because they "appear far." But this success is largely due to the best strategy Sun Tzu ever devised: *Deny your enemy an enemy*.

The "fall" of the Soviet Union was a deception campaign, taken right from the pages of Sun Tzu. By feigning collapse, the Soviet Union effectively denied us an enemy, and provided Washington with a grand excuse to slash military budgets and downsize all elements of our defense posture. By 2000 we were operating under hollow force conditions - our weakest point since before WW II and one of the reasons al Qaeda chose to strike.

We thought the communist economic system finally collapsed, but you should have learned in this book that they never cared about the economy. It did not take 70 years for the Soviet Union to collapse under its own weight. That happened, as it has in every communist nation, within months of their takeover. They have stayed alive all this time *because the West has supported them*!

Thanks to Presidents George W. Bush and Donald Trump, we have worked to rebuild our military, but the Russians have been dismissed as a serious foe. Consider how clever this strategy is. Democrats were able to say, "See, the Russians were never a real threat, we were right all along." Republicans meanwhile, pat themselves on the back for defeating communism. Both declared themselves the victor and went home—leaving the barn door open in the process.

Have we won the Cold War? Did we defeat Communism? Look around you. It is everywhere. Successive African, Central and South American nations are succumbing to it. They never stopped. We just gave up the fight because we thought it was over. Today this notion is ridiculed, but those who do so are people who have invested their careers in the notion that we won, and have a hard time considering that they may have been wrong.

# Back from the Brink: A Comprehensive Plan to Save America

Our nation stands on the precipice. The election of President Donald Trump gave us some breathing room, but with Biden assuming the presidency in 2021—stolen election or not—it wasn't enough. The Left has gone into hyperdrive to prevent another Trump presidency or anything like it. For them it is now or never.

In a certain way, this may have helped us. As it always does, the Left has overplayed its hand. Its motives, behavior and intentions are totally out of the closet. It remains for us to exploit this glaring fact. Our mission is to capitalize on this chance to save our nation and drag us back from the brink of doom. If we fail, it will spell the end of our nation and the world as we know it.

The Left overwhelmingly controls the most important institutions of power: the media (probably the most important), education, Hollywood/popular culture, and much of the federal government and bureaucracies at all levels. Now the military, federal law enforcement, and intelligence agencies too are being overwhelmed. The COVID epidemic has also revealed how entrenched they are in the field of science especially public health agencies like the CDC.

It is truly disheartening. But we should not be demoralized or discouraged. We all got here by ignoring the problem for too long. So now we need to pay attention.


## Create a Parallel Society

We will need to set up a parallel society. The Left's grip on critical institutions like media, education, and the bureaucracy cannot be easily broken head on.

Our constitutional form of government makes alternatives possible, and it has already started to happen. As key red states have proven, people want alternatives to the Left's lunacy. People are flooding out of California and New York for red state havens like Florida and Texas.

Florida is booming due to the strong policies of Governor Ron DeSantis. In Florida, the 2020 election was conducted flawlessly. He has bravely taken on both big tech and the Antifa/BLM movement. He recently signed an anti-rioting law with a warning that in Florida, rioters will face jail. Governor DeSantis is also doing everything within his power to defeat the Left's smothering censorship. Protested by all the usual suspects, most people will cheer these efforts, even though they may not admit it publicly.

As these bold steps are rewarded with increasing support, more leaders are feeling emboldened to do the same. As more and more such policies are adopted, blue states will face a massive hemorrhage of people or a political revival that will throw their leftist leadership out of office.

The parallel society we create will become the preferred society, and as more and more people vote with their feet, the Left will be abandoned by the side of the road. Many of them will choose personal survival over the lunacy they create and reluctantly follow suit. The only danger is that those moving from blue states will bring their ideology with them. If they try to impose it in their new homes, they must be confronted with one question: "Didn't you move here to escape that?"

The five points below as well as some of the key election proposals borrow from Trevor Loudon's "Nine Starter Steps to Save America," an invaluable contribution to the discussion.[219] These are basic steps we all need to take:

1. Face reality. Millions of Americans are still in complete denial. Many think the military is secretly in control—that it's only a matter of time until justice is done and President Donald Trump is restored.

There's a "secret plan"—just "have faith." The truth is that Trump was outmaneuvered by an alliance of communists, globalists, and even traitors in his own party. The "deep state" is now almost fully in control.

2. <u>Resist all violent rhetoric</u>: Violence will not save America. The harsh reality is that President Barack Obama had eight years to replace patriotic generals with left-leaning political appointees. He did a great job. If violence breaks out (God forbid), the military will stand with the government, not the patriots. Furthermore, violent rhetoric may feel good, but it does not help anyone. Remember what Nechayev said, "*increasing the evils and miseries of the people until at last their patience is exhausted and they are driven to a general uprising.*" Feeding that anger only pushes our nation toward the civil war they are trying to provoke.

3. <u>Organize a Compact of Free States</u>. Patriots need to build a "nation within a nation." This doesn't mean secession—our enemies would be quick to exploit such division. What's needed is a reaffirmation of 10th Amendment rights as already outlined in the U.S. Constitution. The already out-of-control federal government is about to go on a rampage against every form of independence left in the country. Every red state with the courage to do so must immediately begin working toward a formal compact to collectively oppose all forms of federal overreach.

   - <u>Every free state should immediately begin adopting the "Republic Review" process</u>, (http://www.reclaimingtherepublic.org/). There's a small but growing movement in some Western and Northern states to review their engagement with the federal

government to eliminate or nullify all
unconstitutional relationships.

- Form a Multi-State 'America First' Popular
  Alliance. The left has "Our Revolution,"
  (https://ourrevolution.com/), a nationwide
  alliance of 600 groups operating both inside
  and outside of the Democratic
  Party. Operated by Democratic Socialists of
  America and the Communist Party USA, Our
  Revolution works in the Democratic
  primaries to elect far-left candidates such as
  Reps. Alexandria Ocasio-Cortez (D-N.Y.),
  Ilhan Omar (D-Minn.), and Rashida Tlaib
  (D-Mich.) into office. Our Revolution isn't
  subject to Democratic Party discipline, but it
  does get to choose Democratic candidates.
  We need an "America First" umbrella group
  to operate both outside and inside the
  Republican Party—even possibly within the
  Democratic Party in some areas.

4. Boycott/Buycott Bigtime. Patriots should be
   abandoning Google, Facebook, Twitter, etc. for more
   honest platforms. They should also enthusiastically
   support efforts by DeSantis to heavily fine Big Tech
   operators who "cancel" patriots. If 25 or 30 free
   states did the same, Big Tech would soon be little
   tech. Patriots need to organize nationwide boycotts
   of unpatriotic companies and buycotts for loyal
   American companies like My Pillow and Goya
   Foods.

5. Remove Malign Foreign Influence at State Level.
   [Florida governor] Ron DeSantis has announced
   legislation to massively curtail Communist Chinese
   activity in Florida.[220] The legislation also targets
   several other enemy states, including Russia, Iran,

Syria, North Korea, Cuba, and Venezuela—all of which interfere in this country's internal affairs.

## All Power Flows Downhill

Good leadership at the top is essential to restoring good leadership at all levels, both within and without government. It is necessary to begin the long process of restoring our constitutional republic. Franklin said, "a republic if you can keep it." Here are the ways to keep it.

**Issues** - Enemies seek to subvert, undermine and sell off our sovereignty. Winning or losing the following agendas will spell salvation or doom:

## Elections

- Restore election integrity in all red states. If voter trust isn't restored within months, the Republican Party is doomed. Thirty states are currently led by Republican legislatures. Some are already holding inquiries into fixing deficient electoral procedures. Most will be whitewashes unless the public gets heavily involved. If the resulting recommendations don't include voter ID and other ballot security, as well as *enforcing* heavy penalties for organized voter fraud, it's likely to be a window-dressing exercise. Be alert. Patriots must work to restore voting integrity first in the red states, then the red counties of the blue states—then after 2022, the whole nation. Get involved in this process. It's a top priority.
- Restore majorities in both houses of Congress in 2022. This is essential to limit the destruction Biden and the Democrats can accomplish. Key to that effort will be to

prevent federalizing elections, which Democrats will attempt with passage of HR. 1, the For the People Act, which federalizes elections, would mandate mail-in voting and ban any voter ID requirement. If passed, it would likely be struck down as unconstitutional, but that may happen too late if it is applied to the 2022 election. West Virginia Democratic Senator Joe Manchin has pledged that he will vote against removing the filibuster. If he caves, it is all over for us

- <u>Close Republican Primaries Immediately</u>. This should be a no-brainer, but no one is talking about it. Only five U.S. states have truly closed Republican primaries. This means that in most states Democrats and independents (even Communists) can vote in Republican primaries— and they do. In many states the GOP's enemies vote in Republican primaries to pick the weakest candidate they can, and sometimes the candidate is actually a Democrat or other leftist who joins the GOP to dilute and undermine GOP political strength. <u>Key Tactic</u>: Don't give campaign donations to national parties: give directly to the candidate or SuperPACs dedicated to the candidate. *Pick good candidates*!

- <u>Maintain and increase majorities in state houses, governorships, and local government</u>. One of President Trump's major accomplishments was to appoint many good judges to federal courts. We saw how corrupt judges allowed Democrats in key states to violate state election law by changing the rules at the last minute. This was one of the biggest reasons they were able to steal the presidential election and senatorial elections in Georgia. With the latter, they got inexcusable help from GOP Governor Brian Kemp and Secretary of State Brad Raffensperger. The GOP needs to do much better

- <u>Elect competent jurists and sheriffs</u>. Many of us overlook state and local judicial elections. The result is more bad decisions from leftist judges. Sheriffs also have immense power in some jurisdictions, where they are the top law enforcement officer in the county. Support the Constitutional Sheriffs and Peace Officers Association (www.CSPOA.org), which seeks to restore the constitutional power sheriffs are supposed to have and still do have in some places. The purpose is to make all of these institutions of government answerable to We the People

- Elect good leaders in local government. Local elections are critical. We tend to overlook them. This is why the Left wins. We need good candidates for school boards, mayors, executives, city/county councils, registrar of voters, judges, and sheriffs. No elective office should be ignored
- Participate in elections as a volunteer, a candidate, or with money if you can
- Create Super PACs. Make alliances with other candidate supporters and raise money
- Support Promising Candidates: Identify and support strong candidates who commit to our issues
- Demand that all candidates take a survey gauging their support for our issues. At the very least, they must commit to those and sign the survey saying so. Preferably they have an existing track record that proves their allegiance
- Advocate civil service reform to enable discipline of bureaucracies wildly out of control
- Combat vote fraud.
  True the Vote (www.truethevote.org)
  Judicial Watch (www.judicialwatch.org)
  Public Interest Legal Foundation
  (https://publicinterestlegal.org/)
  Voter Integrity Project
  (https://voterintegrityproject.com/)
  All do good work in this area. Get involved!
- Develop/join an army of poll watchers/poll judges

- Develop/join an army of precinct captains (<u>Precinct Project</u>)
- Organize and support state Voter Integrity Projects (*e.g.*, VA/MD, NC, CA, & other voting rights groups)
- Volunteer for True the Vote (https://truethevote.org/)
- Demand that voter rolls be purged as required by the NVRA (a step opposed by Democrats)
- Demand prosecution of vote fraud
- Advocate for repeal of NVRA to return full voting discretion to states
- Seek support from our media, Judicial Watch, Voter Integrity Project
- Demand checking green card registrations. Only a few states require citizenship proof
- Take legal action against illegal campaign coordination & other activities

**Education**

- <u>Make public school taxes portable</u>
  State and local taxes used for public education should instead be used to pay tuition for whatever school parents choose for their kids
  Refund education taxes to those who home school
- <u>Replace school boards with solid people</u>
  Boards hire and fire education bureaucrats, who exercise enormous power
  End the lunatic Critical Race Theory, Black Lives Matter, and radical sex education
  Curricula increasingly being injected into public schools
  Restore critical learning skills, the three "Rs"
  Resurrect trade schools. Low-income community leaders have begged for this for years, but are ignored by their Democrat overseers
  Fight Islamization of public schools. After all, Christian groups cannot teach Christianity. Why is Islam being taught?

- The Left controls hundreds of billions in assets through a network of foundations dedicated to their various agendas, which are also funded with billions of dollars in federal, state, and local grants to leftist-run tax-exempt 501.c.3 and c.4 organizations. Almost no conservative organizations receive government funding. Defunding these organizations will destroy them.
- Provide a clearer definition of subversion in federal law and prosecute the insurrectionists. Urge lawmakers to strengthen laws against subversion. Dangers of Communism are acknowledged in federal law, but law is rarely enforced. Enforce the law!
- Recruit candidates who will commit to ending government grants to leftists and support DOJ prosecution of leftwing foundations/organizations engaged in treasonous activities
- Apply RICO law prosecution to George Soros, Open Society Institute, and other foundations that fund subversive organizations and activities
- Sue Pew Charitable Trusts (violated federal law in its creation)
- Apply RICO law prosecution to foundations that act as subversive continuing criminal enterprises
- Formerly conservative foundations have been infiltrated by the Left—remove leftists by retaking boards

**Immigration**

- Oppose amnesty in all forms
- Finish the Wall along the U.S.-Mexican border
- Abolish the refugee program as currently constructed
- End Diversity Visa lottery program
- End chain migration
- End anchor babies
- End Temporary Protected Status
- Enact mandatory E-Verify in all states

- Add nations to State Department State Sponsors of Terror list
- Make English the official language of the U.S.

## Judeo/Christian Culture

- Defend, restore and celebrate our unmatched religious heritage
- Cultural Marxism's goal was to destroy Christianity and the corruption of our society is the direct consequence. We as a nation have largely abandoned God
- Leftist and Islamic allies seek destruction of Judeo/Christian values because it is our greatest source of strength and cultural stability.
- Discourage interfaith dialogue. It facilitates the Koranic Concept of War: detach the enemy from his faith. Christians and Jews are urged to accept Islam, but Islam is not urged to accept Christianity or Judaism
- Support and defend religious liberty under attack - already lost in Europe; on the way out in Canada
- Join a faithful church if you are not a member already. Tithe regularly
- Liberal churches and synagogues are apostates. If you are a member, leave
- Pray daily for the salvation of our nation

## Language

- Restore correct usage of language.
- "Dreamers" are Illegal Aliens. Call them that
- "Dreamers" are adults (all of the so-called dreamers are 19 to over 30 years old). Stop calling them "children"
- Parents who are to blame for bringing DACA youths to the U.S. will be granted citizenship if DACA is legalized
- "Undocumented Immigrants," a nonsense term. Use the correct legal term: *Illegal Aliens*
- Men are men and women are women. Those who have undergone sex reassignment surgery remain their

biological sex. They have simply undergone very extensive cosmetic surgery, augmented with hormone treatment
- Change "Compassion" to "dependency" and "special privilege" when speaking of interest group legislation. That kind of legislation is simply another form of vote buying

## Lawfare

- Countersue the Left
- Battle back against Council on American/Islamic Relations (CAIR), ACLU and other leftist groups' use of lawfare
- Identify legal organizations in this fight:
    American Freedom Law Center
    (https://americanfreedomlawcenter.org)
    FreedomX Law Center (https://freedomxlaw.com/)
    American Center for Law and Justice
    (https://aclj.org/)
    Many others
- Donate to pro-bono legal teams focusing on this fight
- Oppose leftist claims that "civil rights" have precedence over civil liberties *e.g.,* Christian baker examples, Muslims demanding special privileges for Islam

## Media

- Media is the Left's most critical source of power and control. Our ability to message is limited by leftists who suppress news that challenges leftist orthodoxy, and attack, vilify, defame and destroy the reputations of those who disagree with them - especially the most effective and compelling voices
- Media work with groups like the Southern Poverty Law Center, which designates almost all conservative opponents as "haters" or "hate groups." They do not label violent leftwing organizations like Antifa, the Black

Bloc, Black Lives Matter or other groups as either violent or hateful
- Purchase, take over and/or create major media outlet(s), networks or newspapers. (This is already happening to some extent but much more is needed)
- Try to avoid Hollywood productions that glorify the Left. Most Hollywood movies these days contain leftwing political messages. Boycott them. Keep children from them

## Islam

- Support investigation and prosecution of Muslim Brotherhood front organizations subverting our nation
- Oppose Sharia (i.e., a parallel legal system antithetical to the U.S. Constitution)
- Restore sane law enforcement that recognizes Islamic terrorism and trains to confront it
- Restore and support law enforcement training on Islam
- Ban the teaching of Islam in public schools

## Goals

Immediate term

- Take back both houses of Congress in 2022 (prioritize), and support elections of governors, state reps, state senators, judges and local leaders
- Get out the vote in all elections. For example, in Minnesota, extreme left Muslim fascist Keith Ellison became attorney general in 2018 with only a 90,000-vote margin. Hundreds of thousands of registered Republicans did not vote. Had they voted, the Minnesota outcome would have been markedly different
- State GOPs have failed to get out the vote (GOTV) in many places. One reason why Virginia is now blue. Many state Party apparatuses need a serious makeover

## Medium term

- Support the reelection of Donald Trump or another strong candidate in 2024 (prioritize)
- Obtain, maintain or increase majorities in Congress, state houses, judgeships and local government

## Foundational

- Enduring, ongoing effort to raise public awareness regarding the true nature of the threats we face (prioritize), defeat public corruption, restore our culture, faith, and commitment to constitutional republican government and the rule of law

## Prioritize goals:

1. Critical: those we must win
2. Salvageable: those we can win with effort
3. Low hanging fruit: wins easy to accomplish
4. Long-term: agendas we may win if successful with others

**Strategies** - Identify, Expose, confront, subvert, organize, investigate, prosecute, defund, replace

## Tactics in Support of Strategies

### Know Your Enemy

- National Democratic Party
- Democratic Socialists of America (DSA)
- Establishment GOP (not all GOP)
- The "Swamp" - a nickname for corrupt government infrastructure at all levels
- Leftwing organizations, (*e.g.* SPLC, ACLU, NLG, CAP, IPS, IAF, Antifa, Revcom, Refuse Fascism, BLM)

- Islamist organizations: (*e.g.*, CAIR, Muslim Brotherhood, Tablighi Jamaat, Jamaat ul Fuqra, Gulenists)
- Leftwing Foundations (*e.g.*, Soros's Open Society, Ford, Rockefeller and others)
- Obama Foundation/Organizing for Action
- Mass Media (they are not mainstream at all)
- Education Establishment
- The <u>Red-Green Axis</u> (collusion between radical Left and Islamists, domestically and worldwide)

<u>Expose:</u> Campaign of education through speakers, forums, webinars, articles, letters, videos, social media, to citizens, educators and public officials to expose the Left agenda for what it is: violent, unprincipled, terrorist and criminal; a threat to our very existence.

<u>Confront</u>: The Left engages in scorched earth tactics to silence us. They threaten our venues with lawsuits, violence and public humiliation. They engage in violent protests. They seek to enact "Hate Crime" laws that will criminalize our truth-telling. We need to expose and attack these groups and individuals with lawsuits, criminal charges and public humiliation, and seek legislative changes that will strengthen our cause, for example by repealing hate crime laws.

- Democrats and the Left are the true insurrectionists. They are using their media mouthpieces to accuse us of everything that they are doing
- Everything they say is exactly the opposite of the truth. Never let them get away with it
- Ridicule them
- Write letters to the editor regularly, even to liberal papers. If you are not confident on the subject, bone up on it
- Write letters to your representatives. They do listen. Don't just fill out a preprinted postcard

- Call your representatives. Go visit them
- Participate in mass phone calls to legislators, <u>both Republican and Democrat</u>, when objectionable legislation comes up
- Seek criminal convictions for violent protesters and others
- Challenge their narratives in public debate

<u>Subvert</u>: burrow within to disrupt and expose their plans

- Infiltrate enemy organizations
- Expose their various plans
- Create undercover videos (*e.g.*, Project Veritas, https://www.projectveritas.com/. Support their work)
- Attend their marches (Andy Ngo has bravely done this. Support his work: https://www.andy-ngo.com/)
- Develop network of public supporters who will alert us to town halls and other public meetings where we can show up early and pack the house

<u>Investigate & Prosecute</u>: So much of what the left does is criminal. As state and local political, law enforcement and judicial institutions shift to principled, law-abiding control, these people need to face prosecution and conviction. Long sentences for a few of them would end this overnight. They are such cowards that most are unwilling to face any serious consequences for their actions. But as long as the justice system allows it, their insanity will continue and grow.

<u>Replace:</u> This is the most promising strategy. The Left's control of institutions like public education and media is overwhelming. The home-schooling movement is one very good answer to this. But we need much more. Governor DeSantis, South Dakota Governor Noem and a few others have demonstrated the kind of leadership needed. With such leadership, more will be encouraged to follow as our parallel society grows and flourishes.

## Finally

1) Get on your knees—America needs our prayers. Ask God for help

2) Get off your knees and get to work!

3) Get vocal, get active

God bless you and God bless the United States of America!

# Appendix: The Revolutionary Catechism, By Sergey Nechayev

## I. The Duties of the Revolutionary Toward Himself

1. The revolutionary is a doomed man. He has no personal interests, no business affairs, no emotions, no attachments, no property, and no name. Everything in him is wholly absorbed in the single thought and the single passion for revolution.

2. The revolutionary knows that in the very depths of his being, not only in words but also in deeds, he has broken all the bonds which tie him to the social order and the civilized world with all its laws, moralities, and customs, and with all its generally accepted conventions. He is their implacable enemy, and if he continues to live with them it is only in order to destroy them more speedily.

3. The revolutionary despises all doctrines and refuses to accept the mundane sciences, leaving them for future generations. He knows only one science: the science of destruction. For this reason, but only for this reason, he will study mechanics, physics, chemistry, and perhaps medicine. But all day and all night he studies the vital science of human beings, their characteristics and circumstances, and all the phenomena of the present social order. The object is perpetually the same: the surest and quickest way of destroying the whole filthy order.

4. The revolutionary despises public opinion. He despises and hates the existing social morality in all its manifestations. For him, morality is everything which contributes to the triumph of the revolution. Immoral and criminal is everything that stands in its way.

5. The revolutionary is a dedicated man, merciless toward the State and toward the educated classes; and he can expect no mercy from them. Between him and them there exists, declared or concealed, a relentless and irreconcilable war to the death. He must accustom himself to torture.

6. Tyrannical toward himself, he must be tyrannical toward others. All the gentle and enervating sentiments of kinship, love, friendship, gratitude, and even honor, must be suppressed in him and give place to the cold and single-minded passion for revolution. For him, there exists only one pleasure, one consolation, one reward, one satisfaction—the success of the revolution. Night and day he must have but one thought, one aim—merciless destruction. Striving cold-bloodedly and indefatigably toward this end, he must be prepared to destroy himself and to destroy with his own hands everything that stands in the path of the revolution.

7. The nature of the true revolutionary excludes all sentimentality, romanticism, infatuation, and exaltation. All private hatred and revenge must also be excluded. Revolutionary passion, practiced at every moment of the day until it becomes a habit, is to be employed with cold calculation. At all times, and in all places, the revolutionary must obey not his personal impulses, but only those which serve the cause of the revolution.

## II. The Relations of the Revolutionary toward his Comrades

8. The revolutionary can have no friendship or attachment, except for those who have proved by their actions that they, like him, are dedicated to revolution. The degree of friendship, devotion and obligation toward such a comrade is determined solely by the degree of his usefulness to the cause of total revolutionary destruction.

9. It is superfluous to speak of solidarity among revolutionaries. The whole strength of revolutionary work lies in this. Comrades who possess the same revolutionary passion and understanding should, as much as possible, deliberate all important matters together and come to unanimous conclusions. When the plan is finally decided upon, then the revolutionary must rely solely on himself. In carrying out acts of destruction, each one should act alone, never running to another for advice and assistance, except when these are necessary for the furtherance of the plan.

10. All revolutionaries should have under them second- or third-degree revolutionaries—i.e., comrades who are not completely initiated. These should be regarded as part of the common revolutionary capital placed at his disposal. This capital should, of course, be spent as economically as possible in order to derive from it the greatest possible profit. The real revolutionary should regard himself as capital consecrated to the triumph of the revolution; however, he may not personally and alone dispose of that capital without the unanimous consent of the fully initiated comrades.

11. When a comrade is in danger and the question arises whether he should be saved or not saved, the decision must not be arrived at on the basis of sentiment, but solely in the interests of the revolutionary cause. Therefore, it is necessary to weigh carefully the usefulness of the comrade against the expenditure of revolutionary forces necessary to save him, and the decision must be made accordingly.

### III. The Relations of the Revolutionary toward Society

12. The new member, having given proof of his loyalty not by words but by deeds, can be received into the society only by the unanimous agreement of all the members.

13. The revolutionary enters the world of the State, of the privileged classes, of the so-called civilization, and he lives

in this world only for the purpose of bringing about its speedy and total destruction. He is not a revolutionary if he has any sympathy for this world. *He should not hesitate to destroy any position, any place, or any man in this world.* He must hate everyone and everything in it with an equal hatred. All the worse for him if he has any relations with parents, friends, or lovers; *he is no longer a revolutionary if he is swayed by these relationships.*

14. Aiming at implacable revolution, the revolutionary may and frequently must live within society while pretending to be completely different from what he really is, for he must penetrate everywhere, into all the higher and middle-classes, into the houses of commerce, the churches, and the palaces of the aristocracy, and into the worlds of the bureaucracy and literature and the military, and also into the Third Division and the Winter Palace of the Czar.

15. This filthy social order can be split up into several categories. The first category comprises those who must be condemned to death without delay. Comrades should compile a list of those to be condemned according to the relative gravity of their crimes; and the executions should be carried out according to the prepared order.

16. When a list of those who are condemned is made, and the order of execution is prepared, no private sense of outrage should be considered, nor is it necessary to pay attention to the hatred provoked by these people among the comrades or the people. Hatred and the sense of outrage may even be useful insofar as they incite the masses to revolt. It is necessary to be guided only by the relative usefulness of these executions for the sake of revolution. Above all, those who are especially inimical to the revolutionary organization must be destroyed; their violent and sudden deaths will produce the utmost panic in the government, depriving it of its will to action by removing the cleverest and most energetic supporters.

17. The second group comprises those who will be spared for the time being in order that, by a series of monstrous acts, they may drive the people into inevitable revolt.

18. The third category consists of a great many brutes in high positions, distinguished neither by their cleverness nor their energy, while enjoying riches, influence, power, and high positions by virtue of their rank. These must be exploited in every possible way; they must be implicated and embroiled in our affairs, their dirty secrets must be ferreted out, and they must be transformed into slaves. Their power, influence, and connections, their wealth and their energy, will form an inexhaustible treasure and a precious help in all our undertakings.

19. The fourth category comprises ambitious office-holders and liberals of various shades of opinion. The revolutionary must pretend to collaborate with them, blindly following them, while at the same time, prying out their secrets until they are completely in his power. They must be so compromised that there is no way out for them, and then they can be used to create disorder in the State.

20. The fifth category consists of those doctrinaires, conspirators, and revolutionists who cut a great figure on paper or in their cliques. They must be constantly driven on to make compromising declarations: as a result, the majority of them will be destroyed, while a minority will become genuine revolutionaries.

21. The sixth category is especially important: women. They can be divided into three main groups. First, those frivolous, thoughtless, and vapid women, whom we shall use as we use the third and fourth category of men. Second, women who are ardent, capable, and devoted, but whom do not belong to us because they have not yet achieved a passionless and austere revolutionary understanding; these must be used like the men of the fifth category. Finally, there are the women

who are completely on our side—i.e., those who are wholly dedicated and who have accepted our program in its entirety. We should regard these women as the most valuable or our treasures; without their help, we would never succeed.

### IV. The Attitude of the Society toward the People

22. The Society has no aim other than the complete liberation and happiness of the masses—i.e., of the people who live by manual labor. Convinced that their emancipation and the achievement of this happiness can only come about as a result of an all-destroying popular revolt, the Society will use all its resources and energy toward increasing and intensifying the evils and miseries of the people until at last their patience is exhausted and they are driven to a general uprising.

23. By a revolution, the Society does not mean an orderly revolt according to the classic western model—a revolt which always stops short of attacking the rights of property and the traditional social systems of so-called civilization and morality. Until now, such a revolution has always limited itself to the overthrow of one political form in order to replace it by another, thereby attempting to bring about a so-called revolutionary state. The only form of revolution beneficial to the people is one which destroys the entire State to the roots and exterminated all the state traditions, institutions, and classes in Russia.

24. With this end in view, the Society therefore refuses to impose any new organization from above. Any future organization will doubtless work its way through the movement and life of the people; but this is a matter for future generations to decide. Our task is terrible, total, universal, and merciless destruction.

25. Therefore, in drawing closer to the people, we must above all make common cause with those elements of the masses

which, since the foundation of the state of Muscovy, have never ceased to protest, not only in words but in deeds, against everything directly or indirectly connected with the state: against the nobility, the bureaucracy, the clergy, the traders, and the parasitic kulaks. We must unite with the adventurous tribes of brigands, who are the only genuine revolutionaries in Russia.

26. To weld the people into one single unconquerable and all-destructive force—this is our aim, our conspiracy, and our task.


Reproduced from:
https://www.marxists.org/subject/anarchism/nechayev/catechism.htm.

# Endnotes

[1] Dakin Andone, A Minnesota National Guard and police team were shot at in a drive-by shooting, official says," CNN, April 18, 2021, accessed April 25, 2021, https://www.cnn.com/2021/04/18/us/minnesota-national-guard-police-shooting/index.html.

[2] Luis Andres Henao, Nomaan Merchant, Juan Lozano and Adam Geller, "For George Floyd a Complicated Life and a Notorious Death," *Associated Press*, June 10, 2020, accessed April 30, 2021, https://apnews.com/article/a55d2662f200ead0da4fed9e923b60a7.

[3] James Simpson, "The Kavanaugh Allegations Are Psychological Terrorism, And It's Time They End," *The Federalist*, October 3, 2018, accessed May 4, 2021, https://thefederalist.com/2018/10/03/kavanaugh-allegations-psychological-terrorism-time-end/.

[4] The word "utopia" literally means "nowhere" – from ancient Greek *ou*, no, and *topos*, place.

[5] "VIDEO: Obama speech oceans receding, planet healing," *YouTube*. March 2, 2010, accessed May 10, 2021, (https://youtu.be/u2pZSvq9bto).

[6] Quoted from: P.J. O'Rourke, *Give War a Chance: Eyewitness Accounts of Mankind's Struggle Against Tyranny, Injustice, and Alcohol-Free Beer.* (Grove Press, October 2003).

[7] Richard Wurmbrand, *Marx & Satan*. Bartlesville, (Oklahoma: Living Sacrifice Book Company, 1986), 41 - 44.

[8] *Ibid*, 35.

[9] *Ibid*, 33.

[10] The word first came into use in the early 19th century to describe the ideologies of French radicals. Donald F. Busky, *Communism in History and Theory: From Utopian Socialism to the Fall of the Soviet Union*. (Westport: Greenwood Publishing, 2002, 82.

[11] Wurmbrand. *Op. cit.*, 24.

[12] Francis Wheen, *Karl Marx: A Life*. (New York, W. W. Norton & Company, 2000), 10.

[13] Karl Marx. *The Union of Believers with Christ According to John 15: 1-14, Showing its Basis and Essence, its Absolute Necessity, and its Effects.* Marx, Engels Collected Works (MECW). Vol. 1 636. *(*Archiv für die Geschichte des Sozialismus und der Arbeiterbewegung, 1925).

[14] Whittaker Chambers, *Witness*. (Washington, DC., Regnery Paperback Edition, 1987), 9.

[15] Jake, PhD, Jacobs, "How We Lost Our American Values." *Jake Jacobs, Ph.D.* June 28, 2012. (http://jjusa.org/?p=239).

[16] Wurmbrand. *Op. cit.*, 27.

[17] *Ibid*, 42.

[18] Karl Marx and Friedrich Engels, *The Communist Manifesto*, (New York: International Publishers, 1948), 44.

[19] Karl Marx, "The Victory of the Counter-Revolution in Vienna." *Neue Rheinische Zeitung.* No. 136, 1848. Translated by the Marx-Engels Institute. Transcribed for the Internet by director@marx.org, 1994. (http://www.marxists.org/archive/marx/works/1848/11/06.htm).

[20] Fritz Raddatz, *Karl Marx: A Political Biography.* (Boston: Little Brown & Co., 1978), 66.

[21] *Ibid*, 36.

[22] Bakunin, Works, Vol. III, p. 306, as quoted in Marx and Satan, *Op. cit.*, 13.

[23] Wurmbrand, *Op. cit.,* 33-34.

[24] "Marx to Engels in Manchester, London, 8 March, 1855." Marx-Engels Correspondence, 1855. *MECW*, Volume 39, 526. (http://www.marxists.org/archive/marx/works/1855/letters/55_03_08.htm).

[25] Wheen, *Op. cit.* 8.

[26] "Marx to Jenny Marx [wife] in London, Treir, 15 December, 1863." Marx-Engels Correspondence, 1863, MECW, Volume 41, 498. (http://www.marxists.org/archive/marx/works/1863/letters/63_12_15.htm)

[27] *Ibid.*

[28] Jonathan Freedland, "Book Review: A Man of His Time 'Karl Marx,' by Jonathan Sperber." *New York Times.* March 29, 2013, accessed March 3, 2021, (http://www.nytimes.com/2013/03/31/books/review/karl-marx-by-jonathan-sperber.html).

[29] Sylvia Nasar, "The First Marxist - His latest biographer says the man who wrote the Communist Manifesto was unkempt, unreliable and often broke." *New York Times*. May 21, 2000, accessed May 2, 2021, (https://archive.nytimes.com/www.nytimes.com/books/00/05/21/reviews/000521.21nasart.html).

[30] Daniel J. Flynn, *Intellectual Morons: How Ideology Makes Smart People Fall for Stupid Ideas*. (New York: Crown Forum, 2004), 16-17.

[31] Padover, Saul (trans. and ed.), "Introduction: Marx, the Human Side," to Karl Marx, *On Education, Women, and Children*, (New York: McGraw Hill Book Co., 1975), xxv.

[32] Wurmbrand, *Op. cit.*, 34.

[33] Tristram Hunt, *Marx's General: The Revolutionary Life of Friedrich Engels*. Reviewed by Gardner, Dwight. "Fox Hunter, Party Animal, Leftist Warrior," *New York Times*. August 18, 2009, accessed May 2, 2021, (http://www.nytimes.com/2009/08/19/books/19garner.html).

[34] Friedrich Engels, *The Magyar Struggle*, MECW Vol. 8, 227, January 1849, as quoted in *Marxists.org*, accessed March 2, 2020, https://marxists.architexturez.net/archive/marx/works/1849/01/13.htm.

[35] Nasar, *Op. cit.*

[36] Manifesto, *Op. cit.*, 29.

[37] "Fidel Castro," *Spartacus Education*, September 1997 (updated January 2020), Accessed May 6, 2021, https://spartacus-educational.com/COLDcastroF.htm.

[38] "Fidel Castro Net Worth: $900 Million," *Celebrity Net Worth*, accessed May 5, 2021, https://www.celebritynetworth.com/richest-politicians/presidents/fidel-castro-net-worth/.

[39] Humberto Fontova, "Fidel Castro's true wealth." *Human Events*, May 23, 2006, accessed May 1, 2021, https://humanevents.com/2006/05/23/fidel-castros-true-wealth/.

[40] *Ibid.*

[41] Humberto E. Fontova, *Fidel: Hollywood's Favorite Tyrant*, (Washington, DC: Regnery, 2005), 74.

[42] *Ibid*, 75.

[43] Charles Lane, "Opinion: Raúl Castro retires from office — and escapes accountability," *Washington Post*, April 20, 2021, accessed May 7, 2021, https://www.washingtonpost.com/opinions/global-opinions/raul-castro-retires-from-office--and-escapes-

accountability/2021/04/20/9bcd9df8-a1e9-11eb-a774-7b47ceb36ee8_story.html.

[44] James Simpson, "Entrepreneurial Parasites: Why socialists pursue socialism to the ends of the earth," *Truth and Consequences*, October 5, 2009, accessed April 30, 2021, https://truthandcons.blogspot.com/2009/10/entrepreneurial-parasites-why.html.

[45] Nicholas M. Horrock, "F.B.I. ASSERTS CUBA AIDED WEATHERMEN," *New York Times*, October 9, 1977, accessed May 4, 2021, https://www.nytimes.com/1977/10/09/archives/fbi-asserts-cuba-aided-weathermen-secret-data-on-war-protest-years.html.

[46] Sol Stern, "The Bomber as School Reformer: The press—and debate moderators—shouldn't let Bill Ayers and Barack Obama off the hook," *City Journal*, October 6, 2008, accessed May 8, 2021, https://www.city-journal.org/html/bomber-school-reformer-10465.html.

[47] Chesa Boudin, "Op-Ed: I'm keeping San Francisco safer by emptying the jail. My father should be freed too," *LA Times*, May 6, 2020, accessed May 6, 2021, https://www.latimes.com/opinion/story/2020-05-06/mass-incarceration-san-francisco-coronavirus.

[48] John Lahr, "Rough Justice: David Mamet and Theresa Rebeck on crime and punishment," *The New Yorker*, December 10, 2012, accessed May 8, 2021, https://www.newyorker.com/magazine/2012/12/10/rough-justice.

[49] "Another Obama appointee praising communist dictators," *Pleasanton Weekly*, Oct 16, 2009, accessed May 5, 2021, https://www.pleasantonweekly.com/square/2009/10/16/another-obama-appointee-praising-communist-dictators.

[50] Valerie Strauss & Daniel Southerl, "How Many Died? New Evidence Suggests Far Higher Numbers for the Victims of Mao Zedong's Era," *Washington Post,* July 17, 1994, accessed May 5, 2021, https://www.washingtonpost.com/archive/politics/1994/07/17/how-many-died-new-evidence-suggests-far-higher-numbers-for-the-victims-of-mao-zedongs-era/01044df5-03dd-49f4-a453-a033c5287bce/.

[51] Jung Chang, and Jon Halliday, *Mao: The Unknown Story*, (New York: Anchor Books, 2005), Chapter 1.

[52] *Ibid.*

[53] *Ibid*, Chapter 2.

[54] Howard W. French, "The Mao Myth Survives, but Don't Mention its Dark Side," *New York Times*. July 1. 2005, accessed May 12, 2021, https://www.nytimes.com/2005/07/01/world/asia/the-mao-myth-thrives-but-dont-mention-its-dark-side.html.

[55] "Sergey Nechayev." *New World Encyclopedia*. Accessed January 29, 2014. http://www.newworldencyclopedia.org/entry/Sergey_Nechayev.

[56] Sergey Nechayev, "The Revolutionary Catechism," *Marxists.org*, accessed March 3, 2021, http://www.marxists.org/subject/anarchism/nechayev/catechism.htm.

[57] "Nechayev, Sergei Gennadievich." *The Free Dictionary, by Farlex*, accessed January 5, 2021, http://encyclopedia2.thefreedictionary.com/Sergey+Nechayev.

[58] Revolutionary Catechism, Op cit.

[59] Ana Siljak, *Angel of Vengeance: The "Girl Assassin," the Governor of St. Petersburg, and Russia's Revolutionary World*, (New York: St. Martins, 2008), 111.

[60] *Just Assassins: The Culture of Terrorism in Russia*. Evanston, Illinois: Northwestern University Press, 2010. 9-10.

[61] Marco Ceccarelli, "Revolutionary Self-fulfilment? Nihilism, Terrorism and Self-destruction in Fyodor Dostoyevsky's The Devils." AAEH XXII Conference. *Academia.edu*, accessed March 3, 2021, http://www.academia.edu/1713003/Revolutionary_Self-Fulfilment_Nihilism_Terrorism_and_Self-destruction_in_Fyodor_Dostoyevskys_The_Devils.

[62] Arthur Schlesinger, Jr., *The Vital Center: The Politics of Freedom*, (New Brunswick: Transaction Publishers, 1997), 85.

[63] Rod Dreher, "The Possessed," *The American Conservative*, June 19, 2020, accessed May 8, 2021, https://www.theamericanconservative.com/dreher/the-possessed-george-washington-statue-antifa/.

[64] *Just Assassins. Op. cit.* Footnote #40, 21.

[65] Richard McDonough, "Eldridge Cleaver: From Violent Anti-Americanism to Christian Conservativism," *The Postil Magazine*, February 1, 2021, accessed May 12, 2021, https://www.thepostil.com/eldridge-cleaver-from-violent-anti-americanism-to-christian-conservativism/.

[66] *Ibid.*

[67] Mikhail Bakunin, "Letter to Sergey Nechayev," *The Anarchist Library*, June 2, 1870, accessed May 4, 2021, https://theanarchistlibrary.org/library/mikhail-bakunin-letter-to-sergey-nechayev.

[68] *Ibid.*

[69] The so-called "Insurrection" was almost certainly an influence operation conducted by leftists. That small part of the January 6 activities was planned in advance by a group not associated with march planners. Those Trump supporters who entered the Capitol were egged on by these people, while some Trump supporters tried to stop them. See: "Kyle Shideler: Was the violence on Capitol Hill pre-planned?" *Secure Freedom Radio*, January 8, 2021, accessed May 4, 2021, https://www.centerforsecuritypolicy.org/kyle-shideler-was-the-violence-on-capitol-hill-pre-planned/.

[70] There has been considerable controversy over this quote, many critics claiming that Dostoevsky never wrote it. The controversy appears to rest primarily on the book's various English translations of Russian. One of the most popular reads "I asked him, 'without God and immortal life? All things are lawful then, they can do what they like?'" This translator has been accused of attempting to "Westernize" the original Russian text. A more literal recent translation reads "But, I asked, 'how will man be after that? Without God and the future life? It means everything is permitted now; one can do anything?'" Clearly "Without God... everything is permitted," is a reasonable interpretation of the actual text's meaning and an accurate quote, despite widespread secular criticism. See: Andrei I. Volkov, "Dostoevsky Did Say It: A Response to David E. Cortesi (2011)," *The Secular Web*, 2011, accessed April 2, 2021. http://infidels.org/library/modern/andrei_volkov/dostoevsky.html.

[71] Friedrich Engels, "The Magyar Struggle," from Marx/Engels Collected Works Volume 8, p. 227, first published in Neue Rheinische Zeitung No. 194, January 13, 1849, accessed May 4, 2021, https://marxists.architexturez.net/archive/marx/works/1849/01/13.htm

[72] "Larry Grathwohl on Ayers' Plan for American Re-education Camps and the Need to Kill Millions," posted February 27, 2018, at https://www.youtube.com/watch?v=dyKg5gErL18, accessed May 8, 2021. Grathwohl made the assertion in *No Place to Hide: The Strategy and Tactics of Terrorism* (Part V), a 1982 documentary film directed by Dick Quincer.

[73] James Simpson "Conspiracy of the Lemmings: Barack Obama and the Strategy of Manufactured Crisis; Part III," *Truth and Consequences Blog*, October 28, 2008, accessed May 9, 2021,

https://truthandcons.blogspot.com/2008/10/conspiracy-of-lemmings-barack-obama-and.html.

[74] Larry Grathwohl, *Bringing Down America: An FBI Informer with the Weathermen: Second Edition 2013,* Self-published, 2013. Originally published by (New Rochelle: Arlington House, 1976).

[75] "AP: Oklahoma man released early from prison accused in three deaths," *NBC News*, February 24, 2021, accessed May 9, 2021, https://www.nbcnews.com/news/us-news/oklahoma-man-released-early-prison-accused-three-deaths-n1258734.

[76] "AP: 76,000 California inmates to be eligible for earlier release," *NBC News*, May 1, 2021, accessed May 9, 2021, https://www.nbcnews.com/news/us-news/76-000-california-inmates-be-eligible-earlier-release-n1266044.

[77] Julie K. Brown, "Jeffrey Epstein's injuries look more like murder than suicide, noted pathologist says," *Miami Herald*, October 30, 2019, accessed May 9, 2021, https://www.miamiherald.com/news/state/florida/article236809668.html.

[78] Dan Gainor, "George Soros -- the rich man who is hated around the world." *Fox News*. February 27, 2012, updated May 6, 2015, accessed May 1, 2021, http://www.foxnews.com/opinion/2012/02/27/george-soros-rich-man-who-is-hated-around-world/.

[79] *Ibid.*

[80] Dariusz Tolczyk, *See no evil: Literary cover-ups and discoveries of the Soviet camp experience*, (Yale University Press, 1999), 19.

[81] Leggett, George. *The Cheka: Lenin's Political Police*. New York: Oxford University Press, 1986. 114.

[82] Except where otherwise indicated, Stéphane Courtois, et. al. *The Black Book of Communism; 5th Edition*. (Cambridge: Harvard University Press, 2004), 4.

[83] R.J. Rummel, *Statistics of Democide: Genocide and Mass Murder Since 1900*, (Charlottesville: Transaction Publishers and University of Virginia, 1997), Chapter 6.

[84] "Genocides, Politicides, and Other Mass Murder Since 1945, With Stages in 2008." *Genocide Watch.org*. 2020, accessed March 12, 2021, https://www.genocidewatch.com/genocide-and-politicide.

[85] "The Issue of Genocide and Cuba," accessed May 10, 2021, http://www.cubaverdad.net/genocide.htm.

[86] Bhupinder Singh, "Flirting with Revolution for 70 Years," *The India Tribune*, December 20, 1998, accessed May 1, 2021, http://www.tribuneindia.com/1998/98dec20/book.htm#4.

[87] Courtois, et. al. *Op. cit.* 729.

[88] Jason Howerton, "Bill Ayers' Blunt Response When Asked by Megyn Kelly What It Would Take to 'Make You Bomb This Country Again'," *The* Blaze, July 1, 2014, accessed May 1, 2021, https://www.theblaze.com/news/2014/07/01/bill-ayers-blunt-response-when-asked-by-megyn-kelly-what-it-would-take-to-make-you-bomb-this-country-again, Also see, Stanley Kurtz, *Radical-in-Chief: Barack Obama and the Untold Story of American Socialism*, (New York: Simon & Schuster, 2012), 273. Ayers said, "I can't quite imagine putting a bomb in a building today… But I can't imagine entirely dismissing the idea either."

[89] Jonah Goldberg, "TERRORISTS WHO NEVER HAVE TO SAY 'SORRY'," *New York Post*, February 27, 2008, accessed May 5, 2021, https://nypost.com/2008/02/27/terrorists-who-never-have-to-say-sorry/.

[90] Eduard Bernstein, Translated by Edith C. Harvey. *Evolutionary Socialism: A Criticism and Affirmation (Die Voraussetzungen des Socialismus und die Aufgaben der Sozialdemokratie)*. New York: B.W. Heubsch, 1911. xi – xii.

[91] John P. Roche, *The History and Impact of Marxist-Leninist Organizational Theory*, Institute for Foreign Policy Analysis, Foreign Policy Report, April 1984, ix.

[92] "October (Oktyabr) - 10 days that shocked the World," YouTube.com, January 5, 2007, accessed May 10, 2021, https://youtu.be/EgKQTtLTbsg.

[93] Albert Parry, *Terrorism: From Robespierre to the Weather Underground*, (New York: Dover Publications, 2006), 135-136.

[94] V.I. Lenin, *Lessons of the Moscow Uprising*. Collected Works, 4th English Edition, Progress Publishers, Moscow, 1965, 174.

[95] Parry, *Op. cit.*, 136.

[96] Levgold Robert, Review of *Phillip Pomper's "Lenin's Brother: The Origins of the October Revolution."* Norton & Co. *Foreign Affairs*. January/February 2010.

[97] Kelly O'Connell, "Barack & Marx: Why Revolution is the Only Game in Town." *Canada Free Press*, June 22, 2014, accessed April 5, 2021, http://canadafreepress.com/index.php/article/63975.

[98] Charlie Reese, "An Interview with Lenin Through the Magic of Historical Record." *Orlando Sentinel*. April 12, 1985. Accessed July 15, 2017, http://articles.orlandosentinel.com/1985-04-12/news/0290120030_1_lenin-morality-communist.

[99] Peter Kenez, *Cinema and Soviet Society: From the Revolution to the Death of Stalin*, (London and New York: I.B. Tauris, 2001), 139.

[100] Stephen Goode, "Radical Leftovers," *Insight on the News,* November 22, 1999. Accessed May 14, 2021, https://aus.politics.narkive.com/mBYo7Foy/the-immoral-core-of-the-left-how-the-left-will-say-or-do-anything-to-achieve-its-objectives-the.

[101] Reese, "Interview With Lenin," *Op. cit.*

[102] Stephen Koch, *Double Lives: Spies and Writers in the Secret Soviet War of Ideas Against the West*, (New York: The Free Press, 1994), 5-6.

[103] "Stalin's Little Helper," *Times Higher Education*, March 13, 1995, accessed May 5, 2021, http://www.timeshighereducation.co.uk/161826.article.

[104] Koch, *Double Lives, Op. cit.,* 14.

[105] *Ibid*, 19.

[106] Ralph de Toledano, *Cry Havoc: The Great American Bring-down and How it Happened*, (Washington, DC: Anthem Books, 2007), 13.

[107] Robin Phillips, The "Quiet Revolution" of Cultural Marxism, *Robin Phillips*, February 6, 2018, accessed May 1, 2021, https://robinmarkphillips.com/quiet-revolution-cultural-marxism/.

[108] Linda Kimball, "Cultural Marxism," *American Thinker*, February 15, 2007, accessed March 4, 2021, http://www.americanthinker.com/2007/02/cultural_marxism.html.

[109] William Lind, "Who Stole Our Culture?," *WorldNet Daily*, May 24, 2007, accessed May 1, 2021, http://www.wnd.com/2007/05/41737/.

[110] Emily Brooks & Joseph Simonson, "Pete Buttigieg's father was a Marxist professor who lauded the Communist Manifesto," *Washington Examiner*, April 2, 2019, accessed May 4, 2021, https://www.washingtonexaminer.com/news/pete-buttigiegs-father-was-a-marxist-professor-who-lauded-the-communist-manifesto.

[111] Jennifer Crewe, "In Memory of Joseph Buttigieg, Translator of the Complete Prison Notebooks of Antonio Gramsci," *Columbia University Press Blog*, February 11,2019, accessed May 10, 2021, https://www.cupblog.org/2019/02/11/in-memory-of-joseph-buttigieg-translator-of-the-complete-prison-notebooks-of-antonio-gramsci/.

[112] Emergency Committee in Aid of Displaced Foreign Scholars records 1927-1949 [bulk 1933-1945]. Archives and Manuscripts. *New York Public Library.*

[113] "Murrow at the Institute of International Education," *The Life and Work of Edward R. Murrow, an archives exhibit,* Tufts University Digital Collections and Archives, 2008, accessed May 1, 2021, http://dca.lib.tufts.edu/features/murrow/exhibit/iie2.html.

[114] Kline, Malcolm A. "John Dewey & Soviet Progressives." *Accuracy in Academia.* October 28, 2010. http://www.academia.org/john-dewey-soviet-progressives/.

[115] *Ibid.*

[116] Cry Havoc, *Op. cit.*, 10.

[117] *Ibid.*

[118] Ashley Crossman, "Understanding Critical Theory," *ThoughtCo,* October 15, 2019, accessed May 2, 2021, https://www.thoughtco.com/critical-theory-3026623.

[119] Patrick Buchanan, *The Death of the West: How Dying Populations and Immigrant Invasions Imperil Our Country and Civilization,* (New York: St. Martin's Griffin, 2002), 80.

[120] "Political Correctness &Cultural Marxism," *Discover The Networks,* accessed May 11, 2021, https://www.discoverthenetworks.org/organizations/political-correctness-cultural-marxism.

[121] Timothy Matthews, "The Frankfurt School, Conspiracy to Corrupt." *Catholic Insight.* March 2009, accessed May 1, 2021, https://www.scribd.com/document/195491511/The-Frankfurt-School-Conspiracy-to-Corrupt.

[122] Herb Kohl, "Uncommon Differences: On Political Correctness, Core Curriculum and Democracy in Education," *Project MUSE,* Taken from *The Lion and the Unicorn,* Volume 16, Number 1, June 1992, accessed May 3, 2021, http://muse.jhu.edu/journals/uni/summary/v016/16.1.kohl.html, 1-16.

[123] "Theodore Dalrymple > Quotes > Quotable Quote," *goodreads,* accessed April 5, 2021, https://www.goodreads.com/quotes/124952-political-correctness-is-communist-propaganda-writ-small-in-my-study.

[124] Kimball, "Cultural Marxism," *Op. cit.*

[125] Christopher Lane, Ph.D., "Authoritarianism in America; 'The Authoritarian Personality' in 2017, when gaslighting is political,"

*Psychology Today*, February 11, 2017, accessed May 11, 2021, https://www.psychologytoday.com/us/blog/side-effects/201702/authoritarianism-in-america.

[126] "Critical Race Theory," *Discover the Networks*, accessed May 11, 2021, https://www.discoverthenetworks.org/organizations/critical-race-theory.

[127] James Simpson, "Black Criminals, White Victims, and White Guilt," *Accuracy in Media*, February 9, 2015, accessed May 11, 2021, https://www.aim.org/special-report/black-criminals-white-victims-and-white-guilt/.

[128] Matthew Vadum, "ACORN: Puppet Master of Occupy Wall Street," *Frontpage Magazine*, October 10, 2011, accessed May 11, 2021, https://archives.frontpagemag.com/fpm/acorn-puppet-master-occupy-wall-street-matthew-vadum/

[129] Noel Ignatin, "The POC: A Personal Memoir," *Theoretical Review* No. 12, September-October 1979, accessed May 11, 2021, https://www.marxists.org/history/erol/1956-1960/ignatin01.htm.

[130] *The New Abolitionist Society*, accessed May 11, 2021, https://web.archive.org/web/20021204201054fw_/http://www.racetraitor.org/naindex.html.

[131] Matthew Brown, "'White supremacy is terrorism': Biden urges vigilance against home-grown violence after Jan. 6 attack," *USA TODAY*, April 28, 2021, accessed May 11, 2021, https://www.usatoday.com/story/news/politics/2021/04/28/biden-calls-white-supremacy-terrorism-speech-congress/4884034001/.

[132] *Intellectual Morons*, Op. cit., 16-17.

[133] R. Albert Mohler, Jr. "The Age of Polymorphous Perversity, Part One," *Christian Post*, September 20, 2005, accessed May 11, 2021, https://www.christianpost.com/news/the-age-of-polymorphous-perversity-part-one.html.

[134] Terry Rockefeller and Louis Massiah, "Interview with Angela Davis," *Washington University Digital Gateway Texts,* May 24, 1989, Accessed July 20, 2017, http://digital.wustl.edu/e/eii/eiiweb/dav5427.0115.036marc_record_interviewer_process.html.

[135] Herbert Marcuse, "*Repressive Tolerance*," In Wolff, Robert Paul, Barrington Moore, Jr. and Herbert Marcuse, *A Critique of Pure Tolerance*, (Boston, MA: Beacon Press, 1965), accessed July 15, 2017,

http://www.marcuse.org/herbert/pubs/60spubs/1965MarcuseRepressive
ToleranceEng1969edOcr.pdf, 117.

136 *Ibid.*, 119, 120.

137 *Ibid.,* 100, 101.

138 Mie Inouye, "Frances Fox Piven on Why Protesters Must 'Defend Their Ability to Exercise Disruptive Power'," *Jacobin*, June 17, 2020, accessed May 10, 2021, https://www.jacobinmag.com/2020/06/frances-fox-piven-protests-movement-racial-justice.

139 Frances Fox Piven and Richard Cloward, "The Weight of the Poor: A Strategy to End Poverty." *The Nation*, March 8, 2010, accessed May 5, 2021, http://www.thenation.com/article/weight-poor-strategy-end-poverty.

140 Matthew Vadum, *Subversion Inc. How Obama's ACORN Red Shirts are Still Terrorizing and Ripping Off American Taxpayers*, (Washington DC: *WND Books*, 2011), 89.

141 *Ibid.*

142 Piven and Cloward, "Weight of the Poor," *Op. cit.*

143 Richard Poe, "The Cloward-Piven Strategy," *Shannon Brooks*, accessed May 5, 2021, https://shanonbrooks.com/2013/05/cloward-piven-strategy/.

144 Richard Rogin, "Now It's Welfare Lib; Welfare has come to be looked upon as a right and not a hidden shame or a gratuity," *New York Times*, September 27, 1970, SM 16.

145 Sol Stern, "Acorn's Nutty Regime for Cities," *City Journal*, Spring 200, http://www.city-journal.org/html/13_2_acorns_nutty_regime.html.

146 Glenn Beck, "Radio Clips," *GlennBeck.com*, January 6, 2010, accessed May 12, 2021, https://www.glennbeck.com/content/articles/article/198/34681/.

147 Rogin, "Now It's Welfare Lib," *Op. cit.*, 81.

148 Poe, "Cloward-Piven Strategy." *Op. cit.*

149 Stephanie Flanders, Richard Cloward, Welfare Rights Leader, Dies at 74, *New York Times,* Aug. 23, 2001, accessed April 10, 2021, https://www.nytimes.com/2001/08/23/nyregion/richard-cloward-welfare-rights-leader-dies-at-74.html.

150 The Relentless Conservative, "The Democratic Party's Two-Facedness of Race Relations," *Huffington Post*, August 24, 2011,

Updated October 24, 2011, accessed May 5, 2021,
https://www.huffpost.com/entry/the-democratic-partys-two_b_933995.

[151] Piven and Cloward, *Op. cit.*, 517.

[152] Vadum, Subversion, *Op. cit.*, 79.

[153] "Human Service Employees Registration and Voter Education Fund
(Human SERVE)," *Discover the Networks*, accessed April 10, 2021,
http://www.discoverthenetworks.org/printgroupProfile.asp?grpid=7635
.

[154] D. Bradford Hunt, "Redlining." *Chicago Encyclopedia*, accessed
May 1, 2021,
http://www.encyclopedia.chicagohistory.org/pages/1050.html.

[155] "1934—1968 FHA Mortgage Insurance Requirements Utilize
Redlining." *Fair Housing Center of Greater Boston*, accessed May 1,
2021, http://www.bostonfairhousing.org/timeline/1934-1968-FHA-
Redlining.html.

[156] Jeffrey M. Lacker, "Neighborhoods and Banking," *Federal Reserve
Bank of Richmond Economic Quarterly*, Spring 1995, accessed May 5,
2021,
http://richmondfed.org/publications/research/economic_quarterly/1995/
spring/pdf/lacker.pdf.

[157] *Ibid.*

[158] GSEs are private corporations with public purposes created by
Congress to reduce the cost of capital to certain buyers. Fannie Mae,
Ginnie Mae, (Government National Mortgage Association), Freddie
Mac (Federal Home Loan Mortgage Corporation), and Sallie Mae
(Student Loan Marketing Association) are probably the best-known
examples. Their loan guarantees are assumed to be backed by the
federal government and as such they have no viable competitor in the
private market.

[159] "Release: Statement of Franklin D. Raines, Chairman and CEO,
Fannie Mae. Before the House Subcommittee on Capital Markets,
Securities, and Government Sponsored Enterprises." *Committee on
Financial Services – Democrats.* May 16, 2000.
https://web.archive.org/web/20141207004613/http://democrats.financia
lservices.house.gov/banking/51600rai.shtml.

[160] Ed Morrissey, "The quotes that explain the entire financial
meltdown," *Hot Air.* October 12, 2008, accessed May 10, 2021,
http://hotair.com/archives/2008/10/12/the-quotes-that-explain-the-
entire-financial-meltdown/.

[161] Steven A. Holmes, "Fannie Mae Eases Credit to Aid Mortgage Lending," *New York Times,* September 30, 1999, accessed March 3, 2021, http://www.nytimes.com/1999/09/30/business/fannie-mae-eases-credit-to-aid-mortgage-lending.html.

[162] Paul Kengor, Ph. D, *The Communist; Frank Marshall Davis: The Untold Story of Barack Obama's Mentor*, (New York: Mercury Ink, 2011), 283. Also see: "The Unvetted" presented by America's Survival, Inc & AB Independent Productions, *YouTube*, August 19, 2012, accessed March 12, 2021, https://youtu.be/OWKOhA9s7as.

[163] *Ibid.,* 293.

[164] Mo Brooks, "Floor Speech: Obama Administration's War on Police," *U.S. House of Representatives*, Sept. 8, 2016, accessed May 13, 2021, https://justfacts.votesmart.org/public-statement/1130402/obama-administrations-war-on-police.

[165] "Law Enforcement Officers Feloniously Killed," *FBI: UCR*, 2016, accessed May 13, 2021, https://ucr.fbi.gov/leoka/2016/officers-feloniously-killed/tables/table-1.xls.

[166] Bianca Padro Ocasio, "Police group director: Obama caused a 'war on cops'," *Politico*, July 8, 2016, accessed May 13, 2021, https://www.politico.com/story/2016/07/obama-war-on-cops-police-advocacy-group-225291.

[167] Brooks, *Op. cit.*

[168] *Ibid.*

[169] "Law Enforcement Officers Killed and Assaulted (LEOKA)," *FBI Uniform Crime Reports*, accessed May 12, 2021, https://www.fbi.gov/services/cjis/ucr/publications#LEOKA.

[170] "2019 Crime in the United States: Expanded Homicide Data Table 6," *FBI*, accessed May 13, 2021, https://ucr.fbi.gov/crime-in-the-u.s/2019/crime-in-the-u.s.-2019/topic-pages/tables/expanded-homicide-data-table-6.xls.

[171] For 2010-2019, compiled from, "Crime in the United States: Table 43, Arrests by Race and Ethnicity," *FBI*, accessed May 13, 2021. https://www.fbi.gov/services/cjis/ucr/publications.

[172] "Expanded Homicide Offense Counts in the United States," *Federal Bureau of Investigation Crime Data Explorer*, accessed May 13, 2021, https://crime-data-explorer.app.cloud.gov/pages/explorer/crime/shr.

[173] "Homicide Trends in the United States, 1980-2008 Annual Rates for 2009 and 2010," *Bureau of Justice Statistics*, November 2011, accessed May 12, 2021, https://www.bjs.gov/content/pub/pdf/htus8008.pdf.

[174] "COVID-19 early treatment: real-time analysis of 675 studies," *C19Early.com*, accessed May 20, 2012, https://c19early.com/.

[175] "Special Tasks, Memoirs of an unwanted witness-A soviet Spymaster," (New York: Little, Brown and Company, 1994), 172, as quoted in "Leo Szilard," *KeyWiki.org*, https://keywiki.org/Leo_Szilard#cite_note-9.

[176] Trevor Loudon, *White House Reds: Communists, Socialists & Security Risks Running for U.S. President, 2020*, (Independently Published, 2020), 1-21.

[177] *Ibid.*, 21.

[178] Kaelen Deese, "Obama says Biden is 'finishing' the job of his administration," *Washington Examiner*, June 2, 2021, accessed June 2, 2021, https://www.washingtonexaminer.com/news/obama-says-biden-is-finishing-the-job-of-his-administration.

[179] James Simpson, "Reds Exploiting Blacks: The Roots of Black Lives Matter," *Accuracy in Media*, January 12, 2016, accessed May 11, 2021, https://www.aim.org/special-report/reds-exploiting-blacks-the-roots-of-black-lives-matter/.

[180] Vadum, ACORN, *Op. cit.*

[181] Jared Ball, "A Short History of Black Lives Matter," *The Real News Network*, July 23, 2015, accessed May 11, 2021, https://therealnews.com/pcullors0722blacklives.

[182] Tom Kertscher, "Is Black Lives Matter a Marxist movement?" *Politifact*, July 21, 2020, accessed May 13, 2021, https://www.politifact.com/article/2020/jul/21/black-lives-matter-marxist-movement/.

[183] Trevor Loudon, "Confessions of an American Insurrectionist: Communist Tells of 'Joy' at Watching Police Station Burn," *The Epoch Times*, August 8, 2020 Updated: October 12, 2020, accessed May 12, 2021, https://www.theepochtimes.com/confessions-of-an-american-insurrectionist-communist-tells-of-joy-at-watching-police-station-burn_3454854.html.

[184] *Ibid.*

[185] *Ibid.*

186 Ella Kietlinska, "China Ties to US Riots Exposed by Trevor Loudon," *The Epoch Times*, October 8, 2020 Updated: October 12, 2020, Accessed May 12, 2021, https://www.theepochtimes.com/mkt_app/china-ties-to-us-riots-exposed-by-trevor-loudon-2_3531626.html.

187 "Gordon Chang: Communist China's 'Trying to Overthrow the U.S. Government'| American Thought Leaders," *The Epoch Times*, May 8, 2021, accessed May 12, 2021, https://www.youtube.com/watch?v=9TNqdC984Lc.

188 Zach Dorfman, "How Silicon Valley Became a Den of Spies: The West Coast is a growing target of foreign espionage. And it's not ready to fight back," *Politico*, July 27, 2018, accessed November 12, 2018, https://www.politico.com/magazine/story/2018/07/27/silicon-valley-spies-china-russia-219071.

189 Bill Gertz, "China's Intelligence Networks in United States Include 25,000 Spies: Dissident reveals up to 18,000 Americans recruited as Chinese agents," *Washington Free Beacon*, July 11, 2017, accessed November 5, 2018, https://freebeacon.com/national-security/chinas-spy-network-united-states-includes-25000-intelligence-officers/.

190 Libor Jany, "Minneapolis violent crimes soared in 2020 amid pandemic, protests," *StarTribune*, February 6, 2021, accessed May 13, 2021, https://www.startribune.com/minneapolis-violent-crimes-soared-in-2020-amid-pandemic-protests/600019989/.

191 Kyle Shideler, "The Real History of Antifa," *The American Mind*, June 3, 2020, accessed May 10, 2021, https://americanmind.org/salvo/the-real-history-of-antifa/.

192 Lila Thulin, "In the 1980s, a Far-Left, Female-Led Domestic Terrorism Group Bombed the U.S. Capitol," *Smithsonian Magazine*, January 6, 2020, accessed May 10, 2021, https://www.smithsonianmag.com/history/1980s-far-left-female-led-domestic-terrorism-group-bombed-us-capitol-180973904/.

193 "People: Thousand Currents," *Influence Watch*, accessed May 13, 2021, https://www.influencewatch.org/non-profit/thousand-currents/.

194 "How to Form an Affinity Group: The Essential Building Block of Anarchist Organization," *CrimethInc.com*, February 6, 2017, accessed May 13. 2017, https://crimethinc.com/2017/02/06/how-to-form-an-affinity-group-the-essential-building-block-of-anarchist-organization.

195 "Southwest Land Border Encounters," *U.S. Customs and Border Protection*, accessed May 13, 2021,

https://www.cbp.gov/newsroom/stats/southwest-land-border-encounters.

196 "Average Time Pending Cases Have Been Waiting in Immigration Courts as of April 2021, TRACImmigration, April 2021, accessed May13, 2021, https://trac.syr.edu/phptools/immigration/court_backlog/apprep_backlog_avgdays.php.

197 Anna Giaritelli, "Biden administration to fill in gaps in border levees left open after Trump wall construction halted," *Washington Examiner*, May 12, 2021, accessed May 13, 2021, https://www.washingtonexaminer.com/news/biden-administration-to-finish-13-mile-section-of-trumps-border-wall-in-texas.

198 James Simpson, "GOP immigration plan devised by Communist Party," *WND.com*, July 9, 2013, accessed May 12, 2021, https://www.wnd.com/2013/07/gop-immigration-plan-devised-by-communist-party/.

199 James Simpson, "Highly Organized Migrant Caravans Draw Support From Taxpayer-Funded US Groups, UN," *The Epoch Times*, January 5, 2019, accessed May 12, 2021, https://www.theepochtimes.com/highly-organized-migrant-caravans-are-being-supported-by-taxpayer-funded-american-groups-and-the-u-n-and-theyre-using-women-and-children-as-human-shields_2757266.html.

200 *Ibid.*

201 *Ibid.*

202 "Migrant Caravans," *International Office of Migration*, October 13, 2018, accessed May 13, 2021, https://rosanjose.iom.int/site/en/migrant-caravans.

203 James Simpson, *The Red-Green Axis 2.0: An Existential Threat to America and the World*, (Washington, DC: Center for Security Policy Press, 2018), 34.

204 *Ibid.*, 35.

205 Taryn Fivek, "Hope in the Belly of the Beast: NYC Commemoration of Bolshevik Revolution," *All Power to the Soviets*, November 5, 2017, accessed May 13, 2021, https://allpowertothesoviets.wordpress.com/2017/11/05/hope-in-the-belly-of-the-beast-nyc-commemoration-of-bolshevik-revolution/.

206 *Ibid.*, 40.

[207] J.R. Nyquist, "The Secret Speech of General Chi Haotian," *JR Nyquist Blog*, September 11, 2019, https://jrnyquist.blog/2019/09/11/the-secret-speech-of-general-chi-haotian/.

[208] Joseph Mercola, "SARS-CoV-2 – A Biological Warfare Weapon?," *Mercola*, April 26, 2020, accessed April 30, 2021, https://articles.mercola.com/sites/articles/archive/2020/04/26/is-coronavirus-a-biological-weapon.aspx.

[209] "Pandemic: How to Prevent an Outbreak," *Netflix*, 2020, https://www.netflix.com/title/81026143.

[210] "Li Wenliang: 'Wuhan whistleblower' remembered one year on," *BBC*, February 6, 2021, accessed May 2, 2021, https://www.bbc.com/news/world-asia-55963896.

[211] "COVID-19 early treatment: real-time analysis of 614 studies: HCQ for Covid-19," *c19early.com*, accessed May 13, 2021, https://c19hcq.com/.

[212] "The Great Reset is 'one of the greatest threats' to democracy and freedom," *Sky News Australia*, May 7, 2021, accessed May 14, 2021, https://www.msn.com/en-au/news/other/the-great-reset-is-one-of-the-greatest-threats-to-democracy-and-freedom/ar-BB1gt4o6.

[213] See: Simpson, *The Red-Green Axis*. 34.

[214] Sarah Simmons, "Wikileaks founder addresses the death of DNC staffer Seth Rich in Fox News interview," *FOX 5 DC*, August 26, 2016, accessed May12, 2021, https://www.fox5dc.com/news/wikileaks-founder-addresses-death-of-dnc-staffer-seth-rich-in-fox-news-interview.

[215] "Obama tells Russia's Medvedev more flexibility after election," *Reuters*, March 26, 2012, accessed May 12, 2021, https://www.reuters.com/article/us-nuclear-summit-obama-medvedev/obama-tells-russias-medvedev-more-flexibility-after-election-idUSBRE82P0JI20120326.

[216] This information has been taken from *Globalfirepower.com*, accessed May 13, 0121, https://www.globalfirepower.com/countries-comparison-detail.php?country1=united-states-of-america&country2=russia.

[217] John Naughton, "The tech giants, the US and the Chinese spy chips that never were… or were they?," *The Guardian*, October 13, 2018, accessed May 14, 2021,

https://www.theguardian.com/commentisfree/2018/oct/13/tech-giants-us-chinese-spy-chips-bloomberg-supermicro-amazon-apple.

[218] Kris Osborn, "U.S. Air Force Has a Plan to Counter China's Super Lethal 'Satellite-Killer' Weapons," *The National Interest*, October 31, 2016, accessed May 12, 2021, https://nationalinterest.org/blog/the-buzz/us-air-force-has-plan-counter-chinas-super-lethal-satellite-18247.

[219] Trevor Loudon, "A New Zealander's 9 'Starter Steps' to Save America from Socialism," *The Epoch Times*, March 4, 2021, updated March 11, 2021, accessed April 2, 2021, https://www.theepochtimes.com/a-new-zealanders-9-starter-steps-to-save-america-from-socialism_3718917.html.

[220] Andrew Atterbury, "DeSantis and Florida GOP target China after CPAC," *Politico*, March 1, 2021, accessed May 12, 2021, https://www.politico.com/states/florida/story/2021/03/01/desantis-and-florida-gop-target-china-after-cpac-1366303.

Made in the USA
Middletown, DE
12 October 2021